Power,
Corruption,
and Rectitude

Arnold A. Rogow **Harold D. Lasswell**
Stanford University *Yale University*

PRENTICE-HALL, INC. *Englewood Cliffs, New Jersey*

PRENTICE-HALL INTERNATIONAL, INC., London
PRENTICE-HALL OF AUSTRALIA, PTY., LTD., Sydney
PRENTICE-HALL OF CANADA, LTD., Toronto
PRENTICE-HALL FRANCE, S.A.R.L., Paris
PRENTICE-HALL OF JAPAN, INC., Tokyo
PRENTICE-HALL DE MEXICO, S.A., Mexico City

LIBRARY OF CONGRESS
CATALOG CARD NO.
63-18283

PRINTED IN THE UNITED STATES OF AMERICA
C

Acknowledgments

The present inquiry was initiated when the authors were Fellows at the Center for Advanced Study in the Behavioral Sciences, Stanford, California, 1954-55. In the interdisciplinary setting of the Center, informal discussion groups came and went as the Fellows discovered, and rediscovered, problems and methods of investigation. We are aware of the lively interest and helpful comment of many colleagues, among whom we refer especially to the late Clyde Kluckhohn, anthropologist, and Else Frenkel-Brunswik, psychologist. Among political scientists Eugene Burdick was most faithfully associated with the early stages of the enterprise. We are grateful to the directors and officers of the Center for providing research facilities and secretarial services. Mrs. Calista Handwerg assisted us in research and Mrs. Jacqueline Spencer typed a substantial portion of the manuscript. Among colleagues outside the Center we have benefited most from discussions with Paul Tillett.

A.A.R.

H.D.L.

Table of Contents

Chapter One

The Tradition: Power Corrupts

When Lord Acton observed without qualification that "power tends to corrupt and absolute power corrupts absolutely," he found words for one of the deepest convictions of modern liberals and democrats. Based on broad and unstated sentiments, the Acton aphorism instantly took on something of the quality of a law or of a fundamental axiom of mathematics. Everywhere there was a feeling that in the mechanics of achieving power men and institutions acquired some malignancy and the greater the power the greater the degree of malignancy. "Power . . . corrupts . . ." seemed to be the trickle of truth brilliantly squeezed out of a mountain of agreement, sentiment, and experience. The aphorism was immediately incorporated into the doctrinal exercises of the professional philosophers of democratic and liberal outlook. But it went much further. It appealed to the common sense of the citizen at large and became a mandatory article of faith in the public declarations of men of democratic action.

Why do we concern ourselves at this late date with a proposition whose appeal is seemingly so self-evident that liberals and democrats of many lands never dream of opening a debate on the subject? Let us be blunt. We challenge the truth of the unqualified Acton principle. We also impugn the adequacy of the intellectual technique by which it was put forward as a truth of observation. Finally we deplore

1

the consequences for democratic politics of the dogmatic acceptance of the Acton principle.

Before we analyze these consequences, we should make it clear that the term *corruption* in the following pages has two meanings or definitions. The first of these endows the word with the meaning that Acton intended when he wrote "power tends to corrupt. . . ." He was saying, as we shall see, that those who hold power tend to value it above all other values, including rectitude and responsibility, to abuse it, and to justify their immoral acts in terms of their authority and position as if, in Acton's words, "the office sanctifies the holder of it." For Acton as for Hobbes mankind was characterized by "a perpetual and restless desire of Power after power, that ceaseth onely in Death." [1] Convinced that men seek power for its own sake, Acton also believed that no man or institution of power could be relied upon *not* to behave in a corrupt manner.

The other meaning of *corruption*, perhaps one more congenial to the American political temperament, refers to behavior in office that is motivated by a desire for personal material gain. Power is corrupting in this context because it provides the power-holder with maximum temptation and opportunity to line his own pockets at the public's expense. The folklore of American politics, permeated with the suspicion that most politicians are corrupt in this sense, has been responsible for a good deal of legislation designed to promote higher standards of political ethics. Despite these efforts the suspicion remains, and because it has affected political attitudes and institutions, we devote some attention to this second meaning of the term *corruption*.

Although Acton's aphorism referred to power as such rather than venality in office, there is no reason to believe that he regarded the latter as irrelevant to what he called "the moral code" by which people in power should be judged. The "moral code" had long since been defined to exclude venal behavior as well as gross abuse of power, and, indeed, the appeal of "power tends to corrupt . . ." owed much to the fact that it could be, and was, understood to refer to both types of corruption. Seemingly lacking complexity or ambiguity, Acton's observation expressed succinctly one of the oldest and truest notions of

---

[1] Thomas Hobbes, *Leviathan*, Part I, chap. 11.

political thought. No one, including Acton, claimed novelty for the statement. In a letter to Bolingbroke in 1729 Swift said:

> . . . I will venture all I am worth that there is not one human creature in power, who will not be modest enough to confess that he proceeds wholly upon a principle of corruption.[2]

Shakespeare makes Brutus say in *Julius Caesar*: "The Abuse of greatness is when it disjoins Remorse from power."[3] What was unique in Acton's statement was the belief that power *had* to be evil.

Acton composed the statement in a letter to Mandell Creighton, who was the author of a five-volume *History of the Papacy During the Reformation*. Acton had written an extremely critical review of Creighton's work for the *English Historical Review*, of which Creighton was editor. Although Creighton was willing to publish the review, he characterized it as "ill-natured, passionate and almost incoherent." After some correspondence between them, Acton rewrote the review, and the the revised version was published in the issue of 1887.

Acton's declaration that "power tends to corrupt . . ." occurs in a lengthy letter to Creighton written in Cannes, France, on April 5, 1887. Taking issue with Creighton's view of the later mediaeval papacy "as having been tolerant and benevolent," Acton questions whether such an attitude is compatible with "historical Accuracy." Creighton's treatment of the thirteenth and fourteenth century popes, confesses Acton, "struck me exactly as it would strike me to read that the French Terrorists were tolerant and enlightened, and avoided the guilt of blood." The popes of the late Middle Ages, he admonishes Creighton, far from exemplifying tolerance and enlightenment, "instituted a system of Persecution . . . They inflicted, as far as they could, the penalties of death and damnation on everybody who resisted it. They constructed quite a new system of procedure, with unheard of cruelties, for its maintenance."

The essence of Acton's argument is that the "system of Persecution" constitutes "the most conspicuous fact in the history of the mediaeval papacy. . . ." Just as a man is hanged for a particular

---

[2] Quoted in Bertrand de Jouvenel, *On Power; The Natural History of Its Growth*, trans. J. F. Huntington (rev. ed.; Greenford, Eng.: Batchworth Press, 1952), p. 319.

[3] *Julius Caesar*, Act 2, Scene I.

crime irrespective of whether "he is a good husband or a good poet," so it is with institutions, including the papacy. They too must be judged according to particular acts and not in terms of their claims to virtue. "We all agree," Acton continues, "that Calvin was one of the greatest writers, many think him the best religious teacher, in the world. But that one affair of Servetus outweighs the nine folios, and settles, by itself, the reputation he deserves. So with the mediaeval Inquisition and the Popes that founded it and worked it. That is the breaking point, the article of their system by which they stand or fall."

Interpreting Creighton to mean that persons in authority must be judged less harshly than others merely because of the power they possess, Acton informs Creighton

> . . . I cannot accept your canon that we are to judge Pope and King unlike other men, with a favourable presumption that they did no wrong. If there is any presumption it is the other way against holders of power, increasing as the power increases. Historic responsibility has to make up for the want of legal responsibility. Power tends to corrupt and absolute power corrupts absolutely. Great men are almost always bad men, even when they exercise influence and not authority: still more when you super-add the tendency or the certainty of corruption by authority. There is no worse heresy than that the office sanctifies the holder of it.

Although there will always be historians who treat the heroes of history as "examples of morality," Acton insists that the "inflexible integrity of the moral code is . . . the secret of the authority, the dignity, the utility of history." And, he continues,

> If we may debase the currency for the sake of genius, or success, or rank, or reputation, we may debase it for the sake of a man's influence, of his religion, of his party, of the good cause which prospers by his credit and suffers by his disgrace.

Only toward the end of his letter does Acton's firm tone with Creighton relent and become almost conciliatory. "Of course," he reassures Creighton, "I know that you do sometimes censure great men severely." But whatever Creighton's approach to history, Acton continues, "my dogma . . . [is] the general wickedness of men in authority—of Luther and Zwingli and Calvin and Cranmer and Knox, of Mary Stuart and Henry VIII, of Philip II and Elizabeth, of Cromwell and Louis XIV, James and Charles and William, Bossuet and Ken."

For Acton the judgment of history was, above all, moral judgment, from which men in power were no more removed than ordinary mortals. Moreover there was to be no historical presumption of institutional virtue, whether the institutions were religious or secular. Unlike other theorists, notably de Maistre and Burke, Acton did not believe that the heads of religious organizations were less corrupt or even less concerned with power for its own sake than the heads of state. The Actonian "dogma" of "the general wickedness of men in authority" spared neither popes, Protestants, nor potentates.

Although "power tends to corrupt . . ." in 1887 was simply the Acton phrasing of a sentiment firmly and widely held, it remains true that the linkage of power with corruption was unknown to Greek and Roman political science. The Greeks, in particular, held no such view of power or the moral frailty of human nature. Although Plato and Aristotle taught that men could be tyrannical or corrupt rulers, the burden of their political writings was to the effect that a proper choice of men and of institutions could prevent tyranny and corruption. For Plato especially the man of knowledge, by which was meant knowledge of the good, was immune to any corrupting influence.[4]

The power-corruption thesis in the western tradition probably originated with Christianity as part of a larger scheme of thought, which held that human nature in general was base, corrupt, and, in both origin and perpetuity, sinful. The early Christian fathers often observed that the rulers and ordinary people alike valued power and gain above all else, and they expected that mortal beings in authority

---

[4] Leo Strauss has pointed out that Greek political philosophy, unlike modern thought, did not juxtapose justice and coercion, or power and virtue. In the writings of Plato and Aristotle, he suggests, the point is clearly made that if "restraint is as natural to man as is freedom, and restraint must in many cases be forcible restraint in order to be effective, one cannot say that the city is conventional or against nature because it is coercive society. Man is so built that he cannot achieve the perfection of his humanity except by keeping down his lower impulses . . . despotic rule is unjust only if it is applied to beings who can be ruled by persuasion or whose understanding is sufficient: Prospero's rule over Caliban is by nature just. Justice and coercion are not mutually exclusive; in fact, it is not altogether wrong to describe justice as a kind of benevolent coercion. Justice and virtue in general are necessarily a kind of power. To say that power as such is evil or corrupting would therefore amount to saying that virtue is evil or corrupting. While some men are corrupted by wielding power, others are improved by it: 'power will show a man.'" Leo Strauss, *Natural Right and History* (Chicago: University of Chicago Press, 1953), pp. 132-133.

would invariably maximize their interests and advance their positions. In *The City of God* St. Augustine assumes that the lust for power inevitably accompanies political life in the Earthly City; Augustine found ample support in the legend of Romulus and Remus for his view that power-seekers were capable not only of corrupt behavior, but also of murder and fratricide. Eight centuries later St. Thomas Aquinas was led to conclude that power could be tamed only through submission to the word of God and the teachings of the Church.

By the late Middle Ages the bias of early Christianity had become the accepted doctrine of political thought. Although in the age of absolute monarchs and pervasive papal power a certain caution was necessary in any discussion of the nature of politics, the political theory of the time explicitly assigns a high place in political motivation to ambition and lust for power.[5] Several writings of the period anticipated, as a device which would check power-corruption, the modern American formula of separation of powers. The good prince, in the works of Mariana and Poynet, shared the powers of state with wise counselors and advisers, and even so, Poynet noted, the intelligent citizen should be ever alert for evidence of venality and corruption among the governors.

It would be true to say, in short, that the marriage of power and corruption and the birth of separation of powers were sanctified in political theory more than a century before the publication of Montesquieu's *Spirit of the Laws* (1748), to which the origin of separation of powers is usually attributed and by which the founding fathers were supposedly inspired. The appearance in America of separation of powers can be traced back to the Puritan landing in Massachusetts and further back still to Calvin's *Institutes of the Christian Religion* (1536). Calvin instructed his followers that:

> . . . it very rarely happens that kings so rule themselves as never to dissent from what is just and right, or are possessed of so much acuteness and prudence as always to see correctly. Owing therefore to the vices or defects of men, it is safer and more tolerable when several bear rule, that they may thus mutually assist, instruct, and admonish each other, and should any be disposed to go too far, the others are censors and masters to curb his excess. This has already been proved

---

[5] The writings of Machiavelli, especially *The Prince* (1513), reflect this point of view, with the difference that Machiavelli tended to condone motives and acts which Augustine and Aquinas would have regarded as reprehensible.

by experience, and confirmed also by the authority of the Lord himself . . .[6]

The political aspects of power-corruption and separation of powers were developed in detail by several influential writers of the seventeenth century, especially Harrington. The *Oceana* (1656) appeared more than thirty years before Locke's *Two Treatises on Government* and influenced not only Locke (and through Locke, Montesquieu), but also several constitutions of early colonial America.[7]

In other words the suspicion of power and the development of the counterchecking device of separation and balance of power were characteristics of both religious and political thought in America long before the constitutional convention of 1787. As has been noted, the power thesis is an ancient one in political speculation, and it may be as old as Christianity itself. But the true parents of the American tradition and its institutional setting appear to be Calvin and Harrington rather than Locke and Montesquieu; from this point of view the origin of separation of powers owes much more to early religious thought than to early political thought. When the word of God was joined to the voice of experience, as it was by Calvin and the New England Puritans, there was no room for further discussion and debate. Consequently the separation of powers doctrine was a first principle of political wisdom by 1776 and not, in the main, a subject for further inquiry or refined qualification.

The problem for the framers of the Articles of Confederation and the later Constitution was not "How can power be justified?" but "Who should have power, and how can power be distributed in such a way as to permit effective government with no tendency to either despotism or corruption?" The formula they chose was the separation of powers doctrine, especially as it was applied and developed by Harrington, Locke, and Montesquieu. Harrington related political

---

[6] John Calvin, *Institutes of the Christian Religion* (1536), bk. IV, chap. XX, par. 8.

[7] Gooch notes that within forty years of the *Oceana* four colonial constitutions showed "a striking resemblance to its details." G. P. Gooch, *English Democratic Ideas in the Seventeenth Century* (Cambridge, England: The University Press, 1927), p. 307. Harrington's influence on American thought is also discussed in Hugh Francis Russell-Smith, *Harrington and His Oceana* (London: Cambridge University Press, 1914), chaps. 7, 8. See also C. H. Van Tyne, *The Causes of the War of Independence* (Boston: Houghton Mifflin Company, 1922).

power to economic power, and he argued persuasively that political stability depended upon an egalitarian distribution of property. But the good order of the commonwealth was not to be based on economic conditions alone. Harrington insisted on the primacy of the rule of law as incorporated in a written constitution and on the establishment of a tripartite division of government. Enactments were to be framed by an upper house or senate, approved or disapproved by a lower body of the legislature, and enforced by an executive branch or "Magistracy." Moreover, the members of each governmental branch were to hold office for a limited time.

Montesquieu, almost one hundred years later, developed a similar conception of republican government. Eighteenth century admirers of the British constitution comprised the largest number of political philosophers of that age, but the Frenchman was second to none in his outspoken veneration for British principles of government. "One nation there is also in the world," he wrote in his *Spirit of the Laws* (1748),

> that has for the direct end of its constitution political liberty. We shall presently examine the principles on which this liberty is founded; if they are sound, liberty will appear in its highest perfection.[8]

Although Montesquieu's examination of "the principles" was faulty,[9] he argued persuasively, if wrongly, that British political liberty was based on separation of powers. "When the legislative and executive powers are united in the same person," he began his statement of one of the famous "principles,"

> or in the same body of magistrates, there can be no liberty; because apprehension may arise, lest the same monarch or senate should enact tyrannical laws, to execute them in a tyrannical manner . . . there is no liberty, if the judiciary power be not separated from the legislative and executive.[10]

Were the same men or the same body of men to enact the laws, ex-

---

[8] Vol. I, bk. XI, chap. 5.

[9] Montesquieu made the mistake of assuming that "To discover political liberty in a constitution, no great labor is requisite. If we are capable of seeing where it exists, it is soon found, and we need not go far in search of it." Vol. I, bk. XI, chap. 5. Clearly *he* did not go far enough.

[10] Vol. I, bk. XI, chap. 6.

ecute them, and sit in judgment, "there would be," as Montesquieu put it, "an end of everything." [11]

Harrington, Locke, and Montesquieu were a formidable array, but the case for separation of powers did not rest on their writings alone. In the American mind of 1776 the principle of separation offered a safeguard against the inevitable abuses of power which were rooted in human nature, and it provided a check against a possible repetition of the worst evils of British colonial government. Few colonists at the close of the Revolution were willing to argue a principle seemingly founded in nature, logic, and experience. Exponents of "consolidated" government were to have their day, but that day was not yet. There was consequently no great opposition to the incorporation of the separation of powers doctrine in the Articles of Confederation and in a number of state constitutions.

At the national level Congress and the executive divided limited authority, and both were dependent on the states with respect to war, taxation, and commerce powers. At the state level power was divided, in theory, between the legislature and the executive, but in practice the legislature was dominant. In almost every state, as Merriam notes, the executive was hampered by restrictions on his tenure, term, and prerogatives.[12] The legislature, although superior in power to the executive, was itself subject to a variety of checks, balances, and restraints emanating from the universal distrust of authority that was reflected in state constitutions.

The six-year period after 1781 put the theory of separation to a severe trial, although not so much for its philosophical and moral principles as for its practical defects. Many saw no danger in the condition of the states before 1787,[13] but viewed from the perspective of the solid citizenry, the experiment under the Articles was not a happy

---

[11] Vol. I, bk. XI, chap. 6.

[12] C. E. Merriam, *A History of American Political Theories* (New York: The Macmillan Company, 1903), pp. 30-32. In eight states the governor was elected by the legislature; in ten states his term of office was limited to one year; and in only three states was he permitted the veto power.

[13] For many years the standard interpretation of the period was that propounded by John Fiske, *The Critical Period of American History* (1783-1789) (Boston: Houghton Mifflin Company, 1888), but his characterization of the pre-Constitution era as "Drifting Toward Anarchy" (chap. IV) has been challenged by a number of historians.

one. There were complaints that Congress lacked power to raise money for defense and the payment of Revolutionary War debts. Congressional enactments were on occasion ignored by state legislatures, and in a number of states property-holders were disadvantaged by cheap money policies and other measures designed to favor debtor elements. After 1783 there were increasingly bitter disputes between states over boundaries, access to waterways, and the right to levy import and export taxes; since there was no superior body which could adjudicate such disputes, they were settled, to the extent settled at all, by guerilla warfare tactics. Meanwhile the view was widespread abroad that the Confederation was tottering and could not survive a determined attack upon it from within or without.

Consequently among the delegates who assembled in Philadelphia in 1787, ostensibly to amend the Articles of Confederation, there were some who came determined on a thorough revision of the existing governmental system. Alexander Hamilton was the principal protagonist of a "consolidated" form of government based on a strong executive and authoritative upper house of the legislative, but there were a number of others in the convention who were not far removed from his position. The near-Hamiltonians agreed with Gerry of Massachusetts that the "evils we experience flow from the excess of democracy," and, like him, they opposed popular election of the lower house of the legislature. Sherman of Connecticut favored selection of national legislators by state legislatures, on the score that "the people . . . should have as little to do as may be about the government. They want information [and] are constantly liable to be misled." A majority of the delegates supported strong curbs on the powers of the states, and although they differed on details, many favored giving some branch of the national government a veto power over the state legislatures. An important body of delegates favored only minimal reorganization of the existing government, but in the main the tenor of the debates was partial to centralization, hostile to state power, and antimajoritarian.

The philosophy of the convention with regard to human nature and power is relevant to our study and deserves fuller exploration for several reasons. First we argue that with the possible exception of the Civil War the elucidation of American political theory has largely been confined to the era of the constitutional convention and its aftermath. Neither the nineteenth or twentieth centuries are studded with the names of great theories or theorists; it seems as if American political thought has always had a history but no present, and indeed the subject area has been the concern much more of historians than of thinkers and philosophers. As one noted historian has suggested, nineteenth century political thought "since Jefferson has been repetitive and sterile." He goes on to observe that

the one major speculative philosopher, John C. Calhoun, was also the one whose speculations were the most irrelevant to American experience; the one magisterial analysis of the principle of democracy came from the Frenchman, Tocqueville. Story's exposition of the Constitution was innocent of theory, and those who read the ponderous treatises by Lieber, Brownson, Hurd, Pomeroy, and Woolsey found little to nourish the mind and less to elevate the spirit.[14]

Although we do not agree that the constitutional convention was a congregation of profound philosophers, or that the *Federalist Papers* constitute "the single most important document on political theory ever written," we must look back to both as major sources of American political philosophy.

The founding fathers, like modern Americans, entertained no idealistic notions of the "natural" capacities and dispositions of their fellows.[15] Then, as now, the phrase "human nature" conjured up the beast and satyr; it was rarely applied to acts of good will, generosity, or sacrifice. The *Federalist No. 6*, written by James Madison, declares that "men are ambitious, vindictive, and rapacious" and largely governed by "momentary passions and immediate interest." The *Federalist No. 37*, also written by Madison, insists that the "infirmities and depravities of the human character" determine the principal motivations in political life; and in *No. 78*, human nature is regarded as "depraved" and all mankind as prone to "folly and wickedness." Government, therefore, is considered an urgent necessity, "the great-

---

[14] Henry Steele Commager, *The American Mind* (New Haven: Yale University Press, 1950), p. 311, quoted in Morton J. Frisch, "The Architecture of American Political Theory," *Ethics*, LXV, No. 3 (April 1955), 182-183.

[15] The views of the founders, with particular reference to the *Federalist Papers*, are explored in Benjamin F. Wright, "The Federalist on the Nature of Man," *Ethics*, Vol. LIX (January 1949). See also Alpheous T. Mason, "The Federalist—A Split Personality," *American Historical Review*, LVII, No. 3 (April 1952), 625-643.

est of all reflections on human nature" in the words of Madison (*No. 51*). Man must live under government, says Hamilton in *No. 15*, "because the passions of men will not conform to the dictates of reason and justice, without constraint."

These views were generally shared. The so-called "radical" element of the time, which criticized both the theory and achievement of the convention, enjoyed little representation at Philadelphia; its influence at the national level was largely peripheral until the election of 1800. It remains true, however, that the human nature conceptions of Jefferson, Samuel Adams, and Thomas Paine, among others, were different from those of the founders, and these differences were reflected in the prolonged controversy over ratification of the Constitution. Jefferson's confident belief "in the general existence of a moral instinct . . . the brightest gem with which the human character is studded . . ." was the nourishing root of a political philosophy and practice that varied somewhat with the doctrine of the founders and the Federalist party. His views that "morality, compassion, generosity, are innate elements of the human constitution" led him, initially, to criticize the Constitution, especially its theory of power, and later to interpret it in a manner that brought down upon him the authoritative opprobrium of the surviving convention delegates.

A number of distinguished spokesmen did not fully agree with either the Federalists or the Jeffersonians in their views of human nature and power. Perhaps the most important of these was John Adams. Although Adams did not participate in either the drafting of the Constitution or the writing of the *Federalist Papers*, his writings and voluminous correspondence did influence both events. Much of our political and constitutional tradition bears the imprint of his presidential term of office (1797-1801).

Adams' dour and pessimistic view of human nature did not generate confidence in any political system. He was especially fond of confronting the idealists with dyspeptic reminders that man was an animal with an animal's tastes and proclivities. "The love of liberty, you say," he wrote Samuel Adams in 1790,

> is interwoven in the soul of man. So it is, according to La Fontaine, in that of the wolf; and I doubt whether it be much more rational, generous, or social in one than in the other, until in man it is enlightened by experience, reflection, education, and civil and political

institutions, which are at first produced, and constantly supported by a few; that is, by the nobility.[16]

A quarter of a century later he could see no evidence that the enlightenment had taken place; perhaps he was even less hopeful of a future improvement in the nature of man. Writing John Taylor in 1814, he observed

> That the first want of man is his dinner, and the second his girl, were truths well known to every democrat and aristocrat, long before the great philosopher Malthus arose, to think he enlightened the world by the discovery . . . The natural, necessary and unavoidable consequence of all this is, that the multiplication of the population so far transcends the multiplication of the means of subsistence, that the constant labor of nine-tenths of our species will forever be necessary to prevent all of them from starving with hunger, cold, and pestilence. Make all men Newtons, or if you will, Jeffersons, or Taylors, or Randolphs, and they would all perish in a heap.[17]

Although Adams was no democrat, his own private views tending to favor a limited monarchical form of government, he had little faith that any aristocracy could govern without abuse. Unlike many conservatives of his time, such as Hamilton, Adams insisted on a clear balance of powers in the government. The chief magistrate, as he saw it, was to incorporate a monarchical element; a senate or small council was to correspond to the aristocratic principle; and a large assembly was to represent the democratic feature. The proposed division, he argued, was based on "nature" and also closely followed the British constitution, which he praised and admired.

One of his arguments for his conception of stable government rested on a view of history which was rather unusual at the time and which was to foreshadow the future as well as inform the past. There was a tendency in history, he insisted, for the monarch to ally himself with the people against the encroachments of the aristocracy or nobility. The people, therefore, far from being distrustful of the chief executive in the state, should instead regard him as their principal defender against elements that might endanger the commonweal. The absolute monarchy, Adams saw clearly, had enjoyed popular support; in this respect he forecasted the future alliances between strong

[16] Letter to Samuel Adams, 1790, *Works*, VI, 417.
[17] Letter to John Taylor, 1814, *Works*, VI, 516.

or "absolute" presidents, such as Jefferson, Jackson, and the two Roosevelts, and the mass of the American people.

If Adams' insights had been generally shared by the convention delegates in 1787, the resulting Constitution might have been very different. For example, the delegates might have adhered to the proposal in both the Virginia and New Jersey plans that the executive be selected by Congress and that he serve for a fixed term of office. Of course the Constitution as finally adopted was as much a product of expediential considerations as of the delegate's own preferences or points-of-view.

The central problem at Philadelphia was not that of reconciling opposing political philosophies or even the conflicting interests of the "large" and "small" states, but the problem of reconciling conceptions of power that divided individual delegates no less than delegations. The central problem involved simultaneously extending the limit, and limiting the extent, of the new government, in keeping with conventional political theory and recent experience under the Articles of Confederation. On the one hand there was the desire to extend federal authority over the states and to strengthen the ruling position of the educated and property-owning classes. On the other hand there was the desire to limit the ability of government to function as a unified, central agency of coercion. If, in the first instance, there was little desire to return to the laissez-faire of the Confederation, there was, in the second case, even less intention to repeat the experience of George III.

The formula decided upon was the division and separation of powers: the division to apply to the assignment of powers to the states and the central government, respectively; and the separation to apply to balance of powers between the executive, legislative, and judicial departments of the national government. Such a formula, we have already suggested, was consistent with the mainstream of political philosophy in the seventeenth and eighteenth centuries, and it also drew upon the experience of the colonies under the royal governors. It seemed also to be founded in "nature" and to be based on "human nature." Most important of all it appeared to satisfy the central problem of the convention, for the delegates felt the formula would enable the national government to resist the encroachments of the states and still operate effectively in all other respects through the concerted action of its three branches.

The formula of separation of powers appealed to the different interests of the time for different reasons. Those who conceived of government as a necessary enemy of majority liberty thought the formula would sufficiently constrain government to permit freedom. The principle of separation was equally acceptable to those who were more concerned with the problem of tyranny *through* government as a result of a future increase in the suffrage leading to majority rule. From this point of view a divided government was better able to cope with the "tyranny of the majority" than a unified governing system.[18] Finally the formula appealed to those less concerned with strict separation of powers than with the ability of the government to function effectively. In fact if the *Federalist Papers* are any guide, the founders did not intend to carry separation to the point of isolation of the separate branches of government. In reply to critics who argued that the separation of powers was minimal or even entirely absent in the Constitution, the authors of the *Federalist Papers* maintained that no government could function on the principle of *strict* separation. The separation of powers, they argued, was designed to prevent the powers of two departments from becoming merged in one. The three branches could properly be regarded as dependent on each other, with each given the power to check and restrain the other. Similarly, according to the *Federalist* interpretation of the Constitution, the relationship between the states and the central government was to be regarded as one of balance and mutual dependence.

Whether for political or other reasons, it is clear that the *Federalist Papers* underestimated the extent to which division and separation of powers was to dominate the new system of government. The final achievement of the Philadelphia convention was a constitution that contained an almost infinite—we are tempted to say an almost unworkable—number of restrictions on power. John Adams could

---

[18] "In our Governments," Madison wrote Jefferson in 1788, "the real power lies in the majority of the community, and the invasion of private rights is *chiefly* to be apprehended, not from acts of Government contrary to the sense of its constituents, but from acts in which the Government is the mere instrument of the major number of the constituents." *Letters and Other Writings of James Madison,* I, 425.

find eight types of checks and balances in the new governmental system, and his list was not exhaustive.[19]

An analysis of the Constitution as ratified in 1789 demonstrates that, with few exceptions, every major government "power" was divided between two or more agencies or divisions.

Power	*Jurisdiction*
Selection of president	State legislatures
	Electors
	House of Representatives*
Removal of president	House of Representatives
	Senate
Selection of senators	State legislatures
Removal of senators	Senate
Selection of representatives	State electorate
Removal of representatives	House of Representatives
Selection of federal judges	President
	Senate
Removal of federal judges	House of Representatives
	Senate

* "The Person having the greatest Number of Votes (in the Electoral College) shall be the President, if such Number be a Majority of the whole number of Electors appointed; and if there be more than one who have such Majority, and have an equal Number of Votes, then the House of Representatives shall immediately chuse by Ballot one of them for President; and if no Person have a Majority, then from the five highest on the List the said House shall in like Manner chuse the President. But in chusing the President, the Votes shall be taken by States . . ."

Article 2, Section 1.

---

[19] Adams listed the checks and balances as follows:
1. the states and territories against the central government;
2. the House against the Senate;
3. the Executive against the Legislature;
4. the Judiciary against the House, Senate, Executive, and state governments;
5. the Senate against the President in respect to appointments and treaties;
6. the people against their representatives;
7. the state legislatures against the Senate;
8. the electors against the people.

John Adams, *Works* (1814), VI, 467. See also Charles E. Merriam, *A History of American Political Theories* (New York: The Macmillan Company, 1903), pp. 139-140.

Power	Judisdiction
Voting qualifications	State legislatures House of Representatives† Senate†
Appointments to high office	President Senate
Domestic legislation	House Senate President Courts
Treaties	President Senate (two-thirds majority)
Admission of new states	House Senate
Constitutional amendments	House (two-thirds majority) Senate (two-thirds majority) State legislatures or conventions (three-fourths majority)

† "The Times, Places and Manner of holding Elections for Senators and Representatives, shall be prescribed in each State by the Legislature thereof; but the Congress may at any time by Law make or alter such Regulations, except as to the Places of chusing Senators."

Article 1, Section 4.

Amendments to the Constitution since 1789 have not fundamentally altered the constitutional basis of separation of powers. For the most part the principal changes have involved elections: the president and Senate are now popularly chosen, although the operation of the "unit rule" in the electoral college affords the possibility that a popularly elected president might gain only a minority of electoral votes.[20]

Our major concern, however, is not with the analysis of the Constitution but with the operation of separation of powers in the governmental system. We propose to examine the effects of separation of powers at various levels of government, federal and state, and in so doing to demonstrate that the Acton aphorism and the institutional mechanisms it supports have essentially frustrated the popular will, confused responsibility for governmental actions, and retarded the effective formulation of policy at state, national, and international levels.

[20] At least two presidential candidates, Tilden in 1876 and Cleveland in 1888, won the popular election, but were defeated in the electoral college.

Let it be clear that when we refer to "power corrupts" in the present context, we refer not to mere words or to a conventional slogan, but to the palpable consequences of separation of powers for the organization of political life in the United States. For example the failure of political parties to develop into national parties, much less to provide us with a system of party government, is primarily due to separation of powers. The confusion of authority and responsibility which has accompanied the expansion of government is due in large part to separation of powers. Finally the capriciousness and indeterminateness of foreign policy in recent years, reflecting conflicts between the executive and legislative branches, is in our time a major consequence of separation of powers. In these areas alone—and they are by no means the only areas—we have paid a heavy price for ideological convictions and institutional arrangements associated with Montesquieu and Lord Acton.

From the point of view of normative democratic theory the impact of "power tends to corrupt . . ." on the history of political parties has contributed to the obfuscation of party function and responsibility. According to theory parties are to perform a number of important governing roles. They are expected to sharpen issues and formulate policies. They are to provide voters with a choice of programs and candidates committed to programs. The winning party is expected to assume responsibility for government, and the losing party is supposed to criticize governmental decisions intelligently and constructively.

In reality these functions are inadequately performed, or neglected altogether, because there are not two or three parties, but several dozen, each equipped with its own issues, policies, programs, and candidates. As the Committee on Political Parties of the American Political Science Association observed in 1950:

> Historical and other factors have caused the American two-party system to operate as two loose associations of state and local organizations, with very little national machinery and very little national cohesion. As a result, either major party, when in power, is ill-equipped to organize its members in the legislative and the executive branches into a government held together and guided by the party program.[21]

---

[21] "Toward a More Responsible Two-Party System," Supplement to the *American Political Science Review*, Vol. XLIV (September 1950). See also James M. Burns, *The Deadlock of Democracy* (Englewood Cliffs, N.J.: Prentice-Hall, Inc., 1962).

The national political parties are essentially state and local party organizations which come together every four years to nominate candidates for the presidency and vice-presidency. The party organizations in the fifty states are cohesive only in the barest sense. The economic, social, and political conditions that foster localism and the primacy of local solutions insure that the balance of political power at the national level is with the state party organizations. In many states and in entire regions of the country, the term "Republican" or "Democratic" is much less designative of national policy preferences than of historical factors and traditional symbolic loyalties. Moreover candidates and party units who emphasize national policy at the expense of local interests are apt to find themselves, in the end, bereft of party support or position.

Thus at the national level the separation of powers is reflected in the separation of parties; the result is that much legislation owes its success to coalition politics rather than to party politics. A similar situation applies to party organization and function within states. As V. O. Key has observed, parties at the state level do not typically perform the role prescribed for them by democratic theory—that is, the role of keeping state government responsible and of providing policy choices for voters.[22] Within a large proportion of states, he notes,

> only by the most generous characterization may it be said that political parties compete for power . . . More commonly, competition for power takes the form of individual rivalry within the major party rather than group competition between parties . . . With the decay of the party system, the enforcement of accountability for the conduct of state government becomes more and more difficult. Even under the most favorable circumstances a sharp discrimination by the public between the rascals and the others is difficult to achieve.[23]

Party lines are hardly more meaningful within states than within the nation at large, and in many states the core labels "Republican" and "Democratic" are without much significance. Urban Democrats

---

[22] V. O. Key, Jr., *American State Politics* (New York: Alfred A. Knopf, Inc., 1956), especially chap. 3, "Frustration of Party: The Perversion of Separation of Powers." See also William V. Holloway, *State and Local Government in the United States* (New York: McGraw-Hill Book Company, Inc., 1951); Austin F. MacDonald, *State and Local Government in the United States* (New York: Thomas Y. Crowell Company, 1955); William Anderson, *The Nation and the States, Rivals or Partners?* (Minneapolis: University of Minneapolis Press, 1955).

[23] Key, *American State Politics*, pp. 13-14.

in state legislatures are likely to have major differences over legislation with rural Democrats, and small-town Republicans are apt to disagree with Republicans from suburban areas adjoining large cities. In many states urban-rural conflict, in a setting where rural political power predominates, is far more important for the functioning of state government than the existence of political parties. When the allocation of seats and committee assignments within legislatures reflects rural control, urban legislators unite less around party than around the power and policy demands of their underrepresented constituents.

The weakness of political parties can be traced to several causes. The tradition that "power tends to corrupt . . . ," reflected in constitutional requirement, custom, and fixed habit of mind, deprives the party of effective responsibility for government. In many states the most important positions in the state government are voted for separately; as a result the party winning the governorship is unable to organize the state administration.[24] In more than one-third of the states nominations for certain key offices bypass the parties altogether.[25] The bicameral legislature, whose existence owes much to the principle "power tends to corrupt . . . ," defeats the possibility of party responsibility or the fixing of any locus of responsibility.[26] Constitutional and other restrictions on the legislature impede if not prevent effective party coordination of policy. In almost all states the legislatures cannot exercise executive and judicial powers, and in many states the legislative power to tax, to incur indebtedness, and to alter municipal and county jurisdiction is limited.[27]

---

[24] The governor may be a Democrat, the lieutenant governor a Republican, the attorney general a Democrat, the secretary of state a Republican, and so on. The gubernatorial election in Iowa in 1956 resulted in the election of a Democratic governor and a Republican lieutenant governor.

[25] In 1951 approximately seventeen states employed nonpartisan primaries for the nomination of municipal, judicial, and school officials, and in two states legislative candidates were nominated in this fashion. Holloway, *State and Local Government in the United States*, p. 55.

[26] "The dual structure allows shifting responsibility from one house to the other, and this facilitates the enactment, rather than the prevention, of poorly considered measures. One house may pass a measure demanded by constituents with the expectation that this measure will be killed in the second house, or a bill may be enacted with little or no consideration in one house and sent to the other house with the thought (or hope) that the latter will correct all defects." Holloway, *State and Local Government in the United States*, p. 145.

[27] State legislatures do not even possess the power to determine the length of their sessions. Thirty states limit the length of session to a specified number of

Gubernatorial power is also extremely restricted in most states. The governors are constitutionally unable to impose effective leadership on the legislature, and their control of administrative power is partial and incomplete.[28] Appeals to party loyalty, even when supported by threats to withhold patronage, do not insure passage of the governor's own legislative program; no matter how large the party majority, the separation of powers works against policy formulation and coordination at the state executive level. Divided party control, a consequence especially of off-year legislative elections, is the more frequent rule in a majority of states.[29] Whether the governor's party is or is not a numerical majority, the governor in many states can do little more than wait upon the legislature for the passage, in bits and pieces, of his legislative program.

Viewed from his own presumably exalted position, the governor often serves as chief executive or chief administrator in name only. Despite the administrative reorganization movement of recent years, in the larger number of states administrative functions are lodged with independent or semi-independent agencies, boards, commissions, and in some cases, individuals. The inefficiency, waste, and needless duplication of services of such administrative "decentralization" are major charges against it,[30] but we are here mainly concerned with the power irresponsibility and wastage that such "decentraliza-

---

days, ranging from thirty in Colorado to one hundred and fifty in Connecticut and Missouri. MacDonald, *State and Local Government in the United States,* p. 133.

[28] In the opinion of one observer, "So restricted are the administrative powers of the governor that he cannot fairly be held responsible for the management of state affairs." MacDonald, *State and Local Government in the United States,* p. 98.

[29] From 1931-53 the governorship and one or both houses of the legislature were divided between the parties at various times in thirty-one states. The percentage of party division ranged from a "high" of 63.6 per cent in Massachusetts, Nevada, and Connecticut to a "low" of 9.1 per cent in Arizona, Iowa, West Virginia, and Wisconsin. Only fifteen states, mainly in the South, experienced no party division between the governor and legislature over the twenty-two-year period. Key, *American State Politics,* p. 55.

[30] For example prior to 1948 the government of New Jersey was divided among ninety-six administrative agencies, control of which was principally exercised "by a so-called house commission, of which the governor was merely a member." In 1948 New Jersey regrouped the ninety-six agencies into fourteen major departments, but other states continue to follow the older plan. MacDonald, *State and Local Government in the United States,* pp. 102-104.

tion" entails. The various agencies, boards, commissions, and individuals are not always responsible to the governor, the political party, or even the electorate for many decision-making functions they exercise. From this point of view the electoral process, which requires the governor and the political party to "account" to the electorate at regular intervals, promotes an essentially false confrontation. Power which is minutely divided and remote from politics and party cannot be effectively confronted.

Paradoxically the weaknesses of democratic government and of the political party in our time owe much to nineteenth and twentieth century efforts to democratize politics. The election of state officials on separate ballots, the rise of the nonpartisan primary and the direct primary, the initiative, referendum, and recall, and the divorce of policy-making and administration from party and political control— all these developments were essentially reactions to real or imagined oligarchical control of the political process coupled, in some cases, with corruption. In the earlier period of our history the role of bosses and political machines, especially in one-party states, seemed to demonstrate not only that "power tends to corrupt . . . ," but also that politics itself corrupts. "To take it out of politics" or "to keep politics out of this" was to remove or limit opportunities for graft, bribery, and corruption. The solution to the problem of political vice, it was argued, was more democracy, and in an atmosphere in which the term "politician" was regarded as either opprobrious or epithetical, more democracy meant less politics.

In practice, however, there has been neither more democracy nor less politics, nor probably less corruption, in any meaningful sense. The separations within the separation of powers, reflected in the multiplicity of governmental units, has been responsible for the rise of the coordinator or "fixer" whose generic line of descent can be traced to the old-fashioned boss.[31] We do not refer merely to the "5 per center" but to the specialist, within and without the formal political structure, who seeks to coordinate, solicit, or restrict the actions of government in accordance with instructions from clients, including clients within government itself. The divorce of power from party has been followed by the remarriage of power with interest group; as a result governmental decision-making is often less a consequence of

---

[31] Cf. Holloway, *State and Local Government in the United States*, p. 119.

majority party policy than of minority interest group policy.[32] The lobby itself is a response to the fact that when power is divided and party control weak, maximum political effect is gained by applying pressure at key points in the political process.

At the federal level especially the consequences of power division and party weakness have been extreme. The expansion of governmental functions over the last fifty years has been accompanied, on the administrative side, by a haphazard multiplication of agencies with obscure powers and responsibilities. Despite the several reorganizations of the Roosevelt and Truman eras, which were designed to regroup a number of agencies under executive leadership, Congress is still disposed to establish governmental authorities with executive or quasi-executive powers outside the major executive departments. Frequently authority and responsibility are diffused, to the effective detriment of both, by entrusting a function to several departments, agencies, or bureaus. In certain cases, involving particularly health and welfare, transportation, reclamation, and flood control, the creation of separate administrative autonomies has contributed to collective administrative anarchy.

The most typical example of the divorce of power from politics is to be found, of course, in the field of regulation where it has been institutionalized in the form of the independent regulatory commission. Although the commissions were established to perform the regulatory function free of partisan influence and in a mood of *expertise*, it is hardly an exaggeration to suggest that the commissions have been neither independent nor regulatory, nor even, properly speaking, commissions. The president cannot directly supervise the commissions, but he may remove members of certain commissions at his pleasure and dismiss the members of others for causes stated in the relevant statute. The regulatory functions of several commissions have been exercised by or with the concordance of the groups, interests, and organizations which were to be regulated. Finally the variety of powers exercised by the commissions demonstrates that the commissions are much less commissions than complexes of executive,

---

[32] As Schattschneider has observed, "In the economy of democratic government the pressure group is definitely a parasite living on wastage of power exercised by the sovereign majority." E. E. Schattschneider, *The Struggle for Party Government* (College Park, Maryland: University of Maryland Press, 1948), p. 190.

legislative, and judicial power. Almost all commissions exercise legislative or quasi-legislative and judicial or quasi-judicial power, and several perform executive functions, including policy determination and planning.[33]

Our point, however, is not that the commissions contravene the principle of strict separation of powers, but that they reflect it too well in that they exercise regulatory power relatively free of executive and legislative control.

If separation of powers promotes political irresponsibility and anarchy in the field of administration, it tends to promote political irresponsibility and warfare in the area of foreign policy determination. Although Thomas Jefferson, when secretary of state, advised President Washington that "the transaction of business with foreign nations is executive altogether," [34] the Constitution invites the president and Congress to compete for power over the conduct of foreign relations. Historically all wars have witnessed a considerable extension of executive power over foreign affairs, and all peacetime periods have seen Congress asserting or reasserting its power over foreign policy. The present era of peace mixed with war, the interdependence of foreign and domestic policy, and the increasing cost of foreign policy have considerably exacerbated the traditional conflict of power.[35]

Uncertain or deprived of party support, the president, in seeking congressional cooperation, must appeal to symbols, such as "national

[33] Robert E. Cushman, *The Independent Regulatory Commissions* (New York: Oxford University Press, 1941) pp. 2-10. Cushman's collection of "labels" which have been applied to the Interstate Commerce Commission suggests that it is all but impossible to classify the major functions of some commissions. The ICC has been classified by various commissioners, Supreme Court decisions, congressional committees and senators, as a "judicial tribunal," "administrative body," "arm of Congress," "executive body," "purely administrative body," "wholly legislative body," and possessing "only executive power." Cushman, *The Independent Regulatory Commissions*, p. 418.

[34] Daniel S. Cheever and H. Field Haviland, Jr., *American Foreign Policy and the Separation of Powers* (Cambridge: Harvard University Press, 1952), pp. 6-7.

[35] Almost half of the 10,627 bills introduced in the first session of the Eighty-first Congress "had foreign policy implications direct and indirect." The state department registered an interest in 657 of the bills. Richard C. Snyder and Edgar S. Furniss, Jr., *American Foreign Policy* (New York: Holt, Rinehart & Winston, Inc., 1955), p. 412. Congress' control over appropriations, in an era when foreign policy is increasingly concerned with economic and military aid, is a source of difficulty.

interest," which are designed to promote bipartisanship. The manipulation of such symbols is effective in the extent to which congressmen may identify political advantage and the local interests they represent with "national interest." Responsible to a different constituency from the president, the congressman cannot easily disregard local attitudes and pressures, no matter how unenlightened or parochial they may be. Moreover even a minority of congressmen responsive to local attitudes and pressures is sufficient, on many occasions, to alter the course of foreign policy. A few members of key congressional committees, and even a handful of votes on the Senate floor, can decisively affect the substance and conduct of foreign relations.[36]

The administration of foreign policy is entrusted to a number of relatively independent agencies of varying powers and functions. The Export-Import Bank exists to facilitate American exports and imports through loans to foreign governments and enterprises supported by them. The Tariff Commission, which exercises certain quasi-legislative powers, supplies the president and Congress with information concerning international trade and the effect of imports on domestic production. The several economic cooperation administrations, which have been established since 1948, administer United States financial aid to foreign countries. The Atomic Energy Commission participates in the formulation of American policy regarding the international control of atomic energy, and it also engages in the manufacture of atomic weapons and the development of peacetime uses of atomic energy. All these agencies, and others as well, deal with various aspects of foreign policy without much executive supervision. Under law the members of such boards and commissions cannot be dismissed for failure to pursue or implement foreign policy goals as stated by the president.

The major consequence of this separation of powers is that much foreign policy has been inconsistent, irresponsible, and unpredictable. In recent history the two outstanding examples of such foreign policy are the Versailles Treaty and the pre-World War II neutrality legislation, both of them excursions in the politics of vendetta. In the crucial period of the Cold War there have been many instances of confused

---

[36] A Senate minority representing no more than three per cent of the electorate is sufficient to prevent ratification of treaties and agreements. Cheever and Haviland, *American Foreign Policy and the Separation of Powers*, pp. 19-20.

and divided policies and pronouncements reflecting division between the president and Congress: criticisms of the secretary of state and state department officials as pro-Communist; the promotion of the interests of Franco-Spain and Nationalist China by influential blocs in Congress; the criticisms of the aid programs and the rejection of long-term aid commitments; the appropriation under the Marshall plan of more than one billion dollars for the export of cotton and tobacco, at the insistence of senators and congressmen from the South; the support accorded General MacArthur by many Republicans in Congress prior to and after his dismissal; the involvement of Congress in interservice conflicts. At the executive and administrative level there have been several important conflicts of pronouncement and policy: the disputes between the state department and the Economic Cooperation Administration over the administration of the aid programs; the several major disagreements between the successive secretaries of defense and the joint chiefs of staff; the failure of the Tariff Commission and Bureau of Customs to cooperate with the state department in securing tariff reductions.

Such conflict of opinion and policy has served less to clarify issues than to confuse our allies and, perhaps worse, to encourage our enemies. At the congressional level it makes little difference whether temperate, reasonable criticism of foreign policy is sacrificed on behalf of urgent local interests or partisan political advantage; and at the executive-administrative level it is of small concern whether differences are legitimate or illegitimate. Constitution and custom permit an irresponsible as well as responsible separation of powers, and the effects of both are the same. In an age when consistent, predictable foreign policy is demanded of world powers, United States foreign policy too often presents disunity, inconsistency, and indecisiveness.

Another important consequence of separation of powers is that it has forced an increase in the personal and extraconstitutional power of the president. In the conduct of foreign affairs the presidents have sought to promote through personal relations the impression of unity, consistency, and decisiveness in our foreign policy. Presidential participation in the international conferences of heads of state at Yalta, Potsdam, and Geneva, the private letters to Khrushchev, and so on permit the chief executive to take an initiative in foreign affairs that is denied or restricted by congressional interpretation of separation of powers. Inveighing against the results of such conferences and against "secret diplomacy" in general does not alter the fact that the *final* responsibility for foreign policy belongs to neither Congress nor the state department; it belongs to the president alone. "The generalization can be made," it has been observed, "that the nation's major foreign policies have been presidential rather than congressional in origin and conception . . . : Washington's policy of nonentanglement . . . Jefferson's embargo, the Monroe Doctrine, Theodore Roosevelt's 'Big Stick' policy, Wilson's Fourteen Points, the Hoover Moratorium, the Truman Doctrine. . . ." [37]

We are not presently concerned with the merits of these policies or with taking a position on the issue of presidential responsibility for the wars and revolutions of our time. Our major point is that the Constitution separates power over the conduct of foreign relations without also separating responsibility for it. Presidential power over foreign affairs is, in part, a result of the fact that power and responsibility are inextricably connected. The presidents therefore have been bound to resist congressional encroachments on the execution of foreign policy and to restrict congressional participation in the formulation of policy in times of crisis.

This does not mean that Congress should take no part whatever in the conduct of foreign affairs. The strengthening of political parties toward more cohesion and presidential leadership would contribute to the effective coordination of executive and legislative policy in general: it would be possible then to speak of party responsibility for foreign policy. Within Congress the abolition of the filibuster, the confinement of committee powers, and the abandonment of the two-thirds vote requirement for treaties would establish conditions for greater consultation and participation. A self-imposed restriction on irresponsible criticism, which in recent years has made a political plaything of major foreign policy issues, would facilitate cooperation.

The reform of the political parties and Congress would also promote a blending of powers in the formulation of domestic policy. Although foreign policy issues have been more urgent in recent years, historically executive-legislative relations affecting internal affairs have also been strained. Whatever the doctrine of separation of powers

[37] Snyder and Furniss, Jr., *American Foreign Policy*, p. 183.

may imply, the president's ultimate responsibility for policy does not begin at the water's edge. He is accountable to the electorate and posterity for his stewardship of the nation's economic and social welfare, and in passing it may be observed that historians have not dealt kindly with presidents who failed to exercise imaginative and effective leadership.

Indeed it is striking to observe that the presidents who have left their mark on history have been those whose relations with the other branches of government were infrequently harmonious and cordial. Jefferson, Jackson, Lincoln, Cleveland, Wilson, and the two Roosevelts experienced major difficulties with Congress.[38] Jefferson, Jackson, and Franklin D. Roosevelt engaged in important controversies with the Supreme Court.[39] With certain exceptions the less important presidents experienced little or no conflict with the other branches of government.[40] In general presidential attachment to policies of minimal consequence has posed much less a challenge to separation of powers than programs related to war, expansionism, or recovery and reform.

Put another way, the separation of powers doctrine has not been challenged by presidential power *per se*, but by programs which were achieved through the use of presidential power. Such programs, moreover, have reflected democratic aspirations and legitimate conceptions of the public interest. The "strong" presidents, for example, have been, for the most part, champions of the majority against vested interest and entrenched privilege. The programs associated with them—Jeffersonian and Jacksonian Democracy, the Square Deal, the New Freedom, and the New Deal—have been popularly supported, and they have also occasioned the most conflict with separation of powers. Frequently drawing fire from the courts, from Congress, and from strict constitutional constructionists, the "strong" presidents have

---

[38] Cleveland and Franklin D. Roosevelt account for two-thirds of all vetoes cast by presidents. Each vetoed more than 500 bills.

[39] Jefferson and Jackson objected to the assertion, and Roosevelt to the results, of the power of the Supreme Court to determine the constitutionality of executive and legislative enactments.

[40] Relations with Congress and/or the courts are not necessarily the measure of greater or lesser presidential importance. However, the "weak" presidents have had better relations with the other branches than the "strong" presidents.

exerted power less for its own sake than for the sake of programs generated by public demands and needs.

The courts, of course, were not designed to reflect the immediate popular will, but it is a paradox of our history that the executive branch has been as responsive to the majority as the legislative branch, and on occasion, more responsive. As was pointed out earlier, it was the hope, if not the intention, of the founding fathers that the chief executive and the courts would act to restrain majority power. There can be little question that the courts, and especially the Supreme Court, have functioned as a restraint on majoritarianism, but there can be equally little question that the chief executive has often served as the people's advocate.

Although the record is mixed, on the whole the legislative branch has been much more the instrument of local publics than of the national public. Congress' responsiveness to broader national problems has been correlated with strong executive leadership, and when such leadership has been lacking, local and sectional interests have usually had their way. Even the exertion of presidential leadership has not been able to overcome the reluctance of Congress to implement important political and economic rights. The right to vote, to run for office, and to participate in political parties, for example, is not yet subject to uniform national law. Paradoxically in recent years the establishment of basic political and civil rights for minorities has been the achievement not of the popularly elected legislative branch, but of the nonelective judicial branch.[41] Congress has also been less sympathetic than the chief executive to the problems of the urban population and the working class.

The separation of powers doctrine, then, has functioned as a restraint, for good or ill, on majority power, and it is still another paradox that the doctrine should have retained its popularity, at the symbolic level at least, in the face of its adversity to majority interests.

---

[41] The present role of the Supreme Court as a defender of civil rights and liberties against "white supremacy" and McCarthyite legislation is a reminder that the Court's power to check majorities have served the forces of progress as well as those of reaction. The view of the Court as undemocratic, which is still current in some quarters, reflects Jeffersonian views and the manifest opposition of the Court to the regulatory movement of the late nineteenth and early twentieth centuries.

Manifestly the frustrations of majority will have not produced a clamor for the abolition of the Supreme Court or the reform of political parties and Congress. Recent attempts to reconstruct these institutions have been greeted with either indifference or marked antipathy. The economy recommendations of the Hoover Commission have attracted more attention and support than those proposals designed to strengthen executive control. Outside the academies—and not always there either—there appears to be little interest in even limited change in the structure and relations of our power institutions.

Much of this indifference can be traced to ignorance of the functioning of these institutions and to the apathy which attends so many structural problems of the present day. A longer-range explanation, however, would suggest that traditional attitudes toward human nature, power, and government have been modified little during the last century and one-half. Indeed the philosophical and political position of the late eighteenth century American elite forms a substantial portion of the ideology of twentieth century, American mass society.

As already indicated, the suspicion of power and government is based on a suspicion of human nature, and the late eighteenth century view of human nature was less than sanguine and hopeful. But it was mainly a view of human nature in the mass; the elite of the time was more trustful of its own inherent nature and capabilities. The rise of universal suffrage and of mass democracy was not accompanied by a corresponding rise in the evaluation of human ability and potential. Notwithstanding currents of faith and optimism the popular view of human nature has reflected the Calvinist doctrine of original sin, and Americans have sought or anticipated evidence of human frailty and weakness in politics. In the twentieth as in the late eighteenth century in America expressions such as "That's human nature" or "He's only human" usually refer to weak or selfish behavior and rarely to acts of sacrifice, rectitude, and moral worth.[42] Much of our politics has been based on the assumption that human nature is base nature and that the political man embodies human nature writ large.

---

[42] Not long ago a congressman from the Middle West, in a discussion of farm price supports, declared that it was "human nature" for the farmers to demand ninety per cent of parity. Shortly afterward a colleague of his held that attempts to redistribute wealth through taxation were based on the tendency in human nature "to try to take away what the other fellow's got."

Our ostensible political idealism has probably served, at least in part, as a defense mechanism against suspicions of the political self and self-governing institutions. Such suspicions, nevertheless, have been palpable in the political play of attitudes and institutions. They have been projected wholesale onto those who are active in politics and government, taking the form of popular distrust of "politicians" and "bureaucrats," and they are reflected in the persistence of "power corrupts" and separation of powers. In an age of democracy the fear of government is, in essence, a fear of the majority based on a fear of the self. In the modern day of self-government the real meaning of "power tends to corrupt . . ." is not "the rulers may be corrupt," but "I am corrupt," and the reality of separation of powers is "I must be divided against myself."

The consequence of this reality has been a malfunctioning of both power and responsibility in our major political institutions. We shall now proceed to examine the behavioral context in which power has been exercised and to determine whether the "reality" is, in fact, real.

Chapter Two

Critique: The Contextual Approach

In demonstrating that the Acton principle has had unfortunate consequences for American political practice, we have by no means demonstrated that the principle itself is false. Thus far the examination has been confined mainly to the historical and philosophical context in which the principle developed. It may be doubted that by exposing the pedigree of "power tends to corrupt . . ." one can succeed in reducing its life expectancy or in contributing to its senescence. Unfortunately the mortality rate of political principles is highest in the formative years; those that survive the early period usually achieve a permanent middle age, and the Acton principle has long since reached maturity.

Nevertheless the validity of the Acton aphorism can be established by considering the behaviors of power-possessing individuals and institutions the principle describes. Acton himself did not explore the behavioral context, and there have been few attempts to apply his equation to concrete cases of interaction among individuals or institutions, power, and corruption. For most citizens the frequent newspaper accounts of corruption in high places in government and business is confirmation enough. It would be as easy, and as absurd, to conclude from such accounts that the recipients of vicuna coats, deep-freezes, and other "gifts" are exclusively drawn from that section of the population once characterized as "ill-housed, ill-clothed, and ill-fed." In point of fact, little is known about the quality and condition of those men and institutions who employ power for corrupt purposes, and we also know little about the operation of rectitude standards in power environments. What factors predispose an individual or institution to seek power for its own sake? What factors predispose an individual or institution to utilize power for private and corrupt advantage? What factors predispose an individual or institution to reject power for its own sake and to maintain a high standard of honesty and probity in the exercise of power?

It is to these questions and accompanying case materials that we now turn our attention. One cannot hope to deal with all predisposing factors in particular cases or with all cases deserving analysis. Our intention is to deal with some factors of special importance and to specify contours of future and continuing inquiry.

The Biographical Test

We begin by noting that the Acton principle does not fare too well even in that world to which it seems especially suited. With few exceptions the rulers of the ancient world enjoyed a power which, if not absolute, was far greater than that employed by most modern political executives. Unencumbered by constitutions, legislatures, courts, public opinion, or other limiting devices, the monarchs of the pre-Christian and early Christian eras exercised substantial personal authority over the lives and fortunes of their subjects. A distressed populace could resort to revolution or assassination, but these were desperate measures which were only infrequently applied.

The age in which rulers approached an absolute power was not one of absolute corruption. As Franz Neumann and others have observed, for every Nero sunk in corruption and debauchery, there was a Peisistratus whose absolute rule was infinitely less corrupt than that of an eighteenth century constitutional monarch or an Augustus who became more enlightened as his power increased.[1] Trajan, Charlemagne, Frederick the Great, and Charles the Fifth were among the most powerful and least corrupt rulers in history.

Marcus Aurelius is perhaps the most conspicuous example from

---

[1] Franz Neumann, "Approaches to the Study of Political Power," *Political Science Quarterly*, Vol. LXV, No. 2, June 1950. See also Harold D. Lasswell, *Power and Personality* (New York: W. W. Norton & Company, Inc., 1948).

ancient history of a wielder of power that was disciplined by the utmost rectitude. For fourteen years, from 147 to 161 A.D., Marcus shared the throne with Antoninus Pius. When Antoninus died, Marcus insisted that Lucius Verus share the rule with him, not as a junior, which Marcus had been to Antoninus, but as an equal. Following the death of Lucius, Marcus shared power with Commodus. Although a number of his contemporaries were ruthless in their pursuit of power, Marcus conducted himself in accordance with the strictures of his *Meditations*.[2]

It is noteworthy that the Marcuses are overlooked in most writings that impute to human behavior a generalized power drive or will-to-power. The striving for power, which has been alleged to exist by thinkers as disparate as Thomas Hobbes and Alfred Adler, casts the Marcuses of history in the role of freaks. And indeed they are examples of psychological distortion if, as Adler in particular claimed,[3] the will-to-power is the principle directing force in human behavior. Moreover the power urge, if it exists, confirms by half, at least, the Acton principle, for one sense of "power tends to corrupt . . ." is that the possession of power creates an insatiable and ungovernable appetite for greater power. Power "corrupts," in effect, because we are led by instinct or drive to prefer it above all other possible values in the personality system.

Most modern empirical research, however, rejects the premise of an innate power drive in human behavior. The evidence suggests that the crucial factor in any generalization involving the power value is the personality structure of the power-seeker. The central hypothesis about such individuals is that they seek power as compensation for deprivation. The deprivation may be experienced by oneself or by the larger symbols with which one identifies: family, friends, professional or business associates, and ethnic, religious, or national group.

---

[2] E.g., "See thou be not Caesarified, nor take that dye, for there is the possibility. So keep thyself a simple and good man, uncorrupt, dignified, plain, a friend of justice, godfearing, gracious, affectionate, manful in doing thy duty. Strive to be always such as philosophy intended to make thee. Revere the Gods, serve men. This only is the harvest of earthly existence, a righteous disposition and social acts." Quoted from the *Meditations* in F. H. Hayward, *Marcus Aurelius: A Savior of Men* (London: George Allen & Unwin, Ltd., 1953), p. 80.

[3] We refer here to his later writings rather than to his earlier emphasis on the psychic effects of organ inferiority and ego deprivation, especially in early childhood.

The power personalities of history significantly include individuals whose life histories record severe physical or psychic injury; we have reason to believe that many of them sought power as a means of compensating for physical disability, ugliness, impotence, and illegitimacy. In other cases the life histories suggest that the pursuit of power was intimately related to deprivations experienced by symbols incorporated in the self system; we suspect in certain instances that power compensated for low estimates accorded the family, group, or nationality with which identification was made.

Seen from this perspective the power drive functions as a compensatory device for the alleviation of deprivation. But it does not follow that power is never sought in the absence of deprivation or that deprivation always results in a quest for power. If the personal history reflects relatively mild or nonexistent deprivation, we surmise that the interest in power may be less compensatory than purposeful with respect to the establishment of public order policies. At the other extreme deprivation which is especially severe may be beyond compensating, and in that event the expected outcome is not enhancement of the power value relative to other values, but resignation, withdrawal, and, in extreme cases, suicide.

The Acton principle draws attention to a specified attribute of the power drive. Power is corrupting, Acton implied, not because it is sought as compensation for deprivation, but because power itself defines the area in which deprivation and compensation function. For Acton the most extreme deprivation suffered by the power-seeker is lack of power, and the most desired compensation is more power. Unless the power-seeker enjoys absolute power, he is necessarily, in some degree, deprived. "Power tends to corrupt . . ." in effect, because the appetite for power is insatiable, and since all power-seeking relates to personal or institutional ambition, the power employed, whether absolute or not, is apt to be exercised in behalf of selfish advantage.

Analysis of cases does not support these generalities. There is no evidence that power in and of itself tends to corrupt in either sense of the Acton principle. Indeed it is tempting to argue that in American political history power has tended more to ennoble than to corrupt those who have sought it and held it. We have had no president, in the words of Paul Appleby, "of proved depravity," but we have had several whose early careers were not distinguished by conspicuous integrity or ethical prudence. Lincoln, as postmaster in Illinois, was a party to minor frauds on the government through the grant of special favors, and it is worth recalling that Chester A. Arthur first achieved prominence as a machine politician.

RAPID CHANGES IN THE POWER ENVIRONMENT

The case of Chester A. Arthur is of special interest as an example of the possible effects upon the personality of a sudden and rather unexpected increase in power. Arthur was one of the seven vice-presidents who became president through the death of the chief executive. As was the case with most of the others, notably Andrew Johnson, Theodore Roosevelt, and Harry Truman, there was a great lamentation when he succeeded to office following the assassination of Garfield in 1881. But the lamentation proved unjustified. Arthur, was not a distinguished president, but he was capable, honest, and responsible.

Chester Alan Arthur was born in a small Vermont town in 1830 and was the fifth child and first son of a Baptist minister. William Arthur, Chester's father, was a man whose opinions tended to conflict with those of any particular community; as a result the family moved almost constantly during the boy's childhood. One account of Chester as a boy is suggestive of his later career in New York politics. According to a boyhood companion,

> When Chester was a boy, you might see him in the village street after a shower, watching boys build a mud dam across the rivulet in the roadway. Pretty soon he would be ordering this one to bring stones, another sticks, and the others sod and mud to finish the dam; and they would all do his bidding without question. But he took good care not to get any of the dirt on his hands.[4]

After being graduated Phi Beta Kappa from Union College in 1848, Arthur simultaneously taught school and studied for the bar. By 1856 he had discovered that the law as a career interested him much less than politics, and thereafter he held a variety of jobs in New York Republican party organizations. But it was not until 1871 that he achieved public prominence. Largely due to the efforts of Senator Roscoe Conkling, a notorious corruptionist, Arthur was ap-

---

[4] Quoted in G. F. Howe, *Chester A. Arthur; A Quarter-Century of Machine Politics* (New York: Dodd, Mead & Co., 1934), pp. 6-7.

pointed collector of customs for the Port of New York, and it was Conkling again who launched him into national politics. In an effort to placate Conkling, who had supported Grant for a third-term nomination, the Republican national convention selected Arthur as Garfield's running mate in 1880.

The Arthur who entered the White House in late September 1881 was popularly regarded as a Conkling henchman and a convinced spoilsman. Although even his enemies were willing to concede that Arthur was intelligent, genial, and charming, it was widely expected that his tenure of office would transform the White House into the national equivalent of the spoils-ridden New York City customhouse.

There is evidence that Arthur was deeply hurt by these expectations. He had previously shown great sensitivity to adverse criticism, and whenever possible he had attempted to disarm it. He was aware, moreover, that the presidency of the United States was not comparable to the presidency of New York City's Grant Club. Concerned to maintain the dignity and stature of his office, he succeeded in confounding his enemies and not a few of his friends. He terminated relations with a number of spoilsmen and went so far as to refuse the patronage demands of Republican leaders in his own state. He vetoed a substantial pork barrel measure and took action to end corruption in the post office department. But his most notable achievement was the abandonment of his former opposition to civil service reform. The so-called Pendleton Act, which in 1883 established a rudimentary form of the modern civil service, was enacted during his administration.

Manifestly the Acton principle does not apply to Arthur. The rectitude value became more and not less important with the increase of power, notwithstanding the earlier acceptance and partial indulgence of corrupt practices. Although it is too much to say that Arthur was ennobled by power, it is quite clear that he was not corrupted in either sense of the Acton principle.

Arthur's rise to national power and eminence was, as noted, rapid. Five presidents have experienced a sudden decrease in power as a consequence of defeat for re-election,[5] but in only one case did defeat

---

[5] We do not include Grover Cleveland, who was defeated for re-election in 1888, but who won a second term in 1892.

result in relative oblivion. John Quincy Adams, Taft, and Hoover exercised influence for many years after their presidential terms of office. Adams, it will be recalled, continued to serve his country as a Massachusetts congressman; Taft was chief justice of the Supreme Court for almost a decade; and Hoover filled numerous positions of trust and responsibility. Harrison was obscure, to be sure, but he did not survive his defeat in 1892 by more than nine years. Martin Van Buren, however, was compulsorily and permanently retired from public office when he was only fifty-eight years of age. A determined power-seeker, he apparently believed that he would be returned to the White House at a later time. But he was not a serious contender in any one of the five elections that transpired between his defeat in 1840 and his death in 1862.

Van Buren's history reflects an intimate relationship between power and personality.[6] He seems to have been interested in a political career from a very early age, and it is quite clear that his tenure of the presidency had been, in his own words, "my most earnest desire" for almost four decades preceding his election. Until his defeat by Harrison he was usually in office or a candidate for office: he served as state senator in the New York legislature, attorney general and governor of New York, United States senator, ambassador to Great Britain, secretary of state, vice-president, and president.

He was a shrewd and opportunistic office-seeker with a sharp eye for the main chance. Although he preferred the company of wealth and aristocracy here and abroad and went to considerable lengths to imitate the life styles of the upper classes, he was a self-styled spokesman of the ordinary citizens in the rising democratic ferment of the period. There is little evidence that he had enthusiasm for Jackson's egalitarian convictions, but he was an early supporter of Jackson and served under him as secretary of state and vice-president.

Van Buren's deviousness and manipulative skill in politics earned him a reputation as a consummate, if somewhat unsavory, politician. In his own time his name was synonymous with intrigue; he was often referred to as "the Little Magician," "the Red Fox of

[6] Studies of Van Buren's life and career include William L. Mackenzie, *The Life and Times of Martin Van Buren* (Boston: Cooke & Co., 1846); Edward M. Shepard, *American Statesman: Martin Van Buren* (Boston: Houghton Mifflin Company, 1888); and Holmes Alexander, *The American Talleyrand* (New York: Harper & Row, Publishers, 1935).

Kinderhook," or "the American Talleyrand"—titles which are suggestive of his reputation. An obituary account in *The New York Times* associated him with Machiavelli and Mephistopheles. Some portion of this implied obliquity, however, was undeserved. Measured against the typical standards and practices of his era, Van Buren was not corrupt,[7] nor was his pursuit of power totally unrestrained. He resisted a number of popular pressures with respect to the financing of internal improvements and his handling of the panic of 1839. It is also clear that had he not opposed the annexation of Texas, he might have won the Democratic nomination in 1844. There were also other occasions when Van Buren displayed courage and allegiance to principle.

His political careerism is unquestionably related to a background of early deprivation. Van Buren, who was born in 1782, began life as the son of a relatively impoverished farmer and tavern keeper in Kinderhook, New York. In his *Autobiography* Van Buren does not refer to the tavern or to certain other facts concerning his origin. The first Van Buren in America was apparently an indentured servant, and there is no proof that any of his descendants, except the eighth president, achieved even a modicum of success in life. But Van Buren tells us that "all" his ancestors held "respectable positions" and were "unblemished characters." In his retirement he was able to obtain from Holland, by methods not known, an ancestral coat of arms which he displayed prominently in his home.

The Kinderhook tavern, moreover, was involved in a rumor connected with Van Buren's birth, which John Quincy Adams helped to immortalize by including in his *Diary*. It was widely speculated that Van Buren was the illegitimate son of Aaron Burr. Burr had frequented the tavern both before and after Van Buren's birth, and it was said that he was not averse to tavern maids or even the wives of tavern owners. There was also, as contemporary portraits show, a remarkable physical resemblance between Burr and Van Buren. It is almost certain that the gossip was without foundation, but it is clear

---

[7] Van Buren's post-presidential life as a well-to-do country squire aroused suspicions among his contemporaries that he had employed his office for personal gain. There is no evidence of this. His comfortable circumstances were probably derived from fees earned in legal practice and from his savings of approximately half his salary during his presidential term.

that Van Buren had good reasons not to assign the tavern a conspicuous place in his early life.

Van Buren may have learned his first political wisdom indirectly
from his father. Abraham Van Buren, the tavern keeper, owed some
of his difficulties in life to a talent for nonconformity. Prior to the
Revolution he had been a Whig when most of his neighbors were
Tories; following the war he embraced Republican principles, although Kinderhook and its environs were strongly Federalist. He appears also to have been a particularly impractical and improvident
idealist, a devotee of lost causes and hopeless schemes. It should be
noted that it was in the antithesis of those qualities—that is, in conformity, practicality, prudence, and realism—that his son excelled.

But Van Buren's foremost talent was the pursuit of power, and
for almost forty years he enjoyed considerable success in obtaining it.
There can be no question that power served a variety of his personal
needs—not least the need to overcome the obscurity of his Kinderhook background—and there can be equally no question that he
found powerlessness almost intolerable. Of all the presidents his fall
from power was perhaps the most abrupt, but the road from Washington back to Kinderhook produced a bitter man rather than a corrupt
one. It may well have been bitterness—certainly it was not corruption
—which led him to decline the final opportunity offered him to exert
influence. It was also his last opportunity to achieve a measure of last-
ing fame. In April 1861, ex-President Franklin Pierce suggested that
Van Buren, as the oldest ex-president, call a meeting of the five living
former presidents to discuss ways of averting the Civil War. Van
Buren declined the suggestion. He died fifteen months later.

That Van Buren was ambitious, and in large measure opportunistic, there can be no doubt. It is also clear that Van Buren's early life
generated demands upon the environment which power was able to
satisfy; in achieving power Van Buren also achieved the eminence,
respect, and material well-being which were denied in Kinderhook.
There is a sense in which Van Buren's power-seeking was compulsive,
but there is no sense in which his quest for power was unscrupulous,
ruthless, or corrupt. The important point is that Van Buren's ambitions did not disfigure his tenure of high office; nor did his opportunism undermine all adherence to principle. Van Buren's history

suggests that even when power is assiduously sought and enjoyed, it is not necessarily corrupting.

The histories of Chester A. Arthur and Martin Van Buren support the hypothesis that relatively sudden shifts of power need not be accompanied by corruption. Indeed in the case of Arthur a rapid increase in power was followed by increased rectitude. Conventionally viewed, the political career of Aaron Burr would appear to suggest that the deprivation of power *per se* can occasion a corrupt response (the so-called Burr conspiracy). Analysis of the available data, however, does not indicate that Burr's career is grist for the Acton mill.

Certainly the riddle of Burr's life has not been and perhaps never will be completely solved.[8] The bafflement once expressed by John Adams is a continuing affliction in any examination of Burr's career, both before and after the famous duel with Hamilton. "I have never known, in any country," Adams declared in 1815, "the prejudice in favor of birth, parentage, and descent more conspicuous than in the instance of Colonel Burr." Fifteen years earlier Burr had barely missed becoming president of the United States. At the time of Adams' remark he was a refugee from his own country, and so far as public opinion was concerned, a traitor and murderer. Although we can probe more deeply than Adams into Burr's life, we cannot hope to uncover all the factors which are relevant to one of the great political mysteries of American history.

Aaron Burr was born in 1756, the second child and the first son of the Reverend Aaron Burr, president of Princeton University. His mother, Esther, was a daughter of the famed Jonathan Edwards. The parents were devoted to each other, and there is evidence that the Burr home was a happy one during the son's infancy. But at the age of two he was suddenly orphaned by a smallpox epidemic; indeed within one year Aaron lost his father, mother, grandfather and grandmother (Jonathan and Sarah Edwards), and great-grandfather.

---

[8] The definitive biography of Burr is Nathan Schachner, *Aaron Burr* (New York: J. B. Lippincott Co., 1937) to which we are indebted for much of what follows. See also Holmes Alexander, *Aaron Burr: The Proud Pretender* (New York: Harper & Row, Publishers, 1937). The best short account of Burr's life and the Burr-Hamilton relationship is Harold C. Syrett, Jean G. Cooke, and Willard M. Wallace, *Interview in Weehawken* (Middletown, Conn.: Wesleyan University Press, 1960).

The two Burr children became wards of their uncle, the Reverend Timothy Edwards. Aaron appears to have been rather unhappy in the new surroundings. The Reverend Edwards, an archetypal Puritan, was pious, strict, and a firm disciplinarian. It is clear that Aaron left home several times, and had he succeeded on one occasion in joining a ship that was preparing to embark from New York, his personal history and the history of the United States would almost certainly have been different.

Young Aaron was educated by private tutors, and at the age of eleven he was sufficiently qualified to apply to Princeton. The college refused to admit him, apparently because of his age and physical immaturity; but two years later, at the age of thirteen, he was enrolled as a sophomore. He was frequently ill during his college days, and when he was graduated in 1772, he left behind a record of scholarship which was good, but not outstanding.

Burr's legal studies were interrupted by the battle of Lexington, and soon thereafter he obtained an officer's commission in forces which were then being led by Colonel Benedict Arnold. Burr took part in a number of battles, notably the assault on Quebec, but his war record is rather confused. He was an aide at various times to Generals Washington, Putnam, and Montgomery, but his service to Washington, which has been the subject of numerous stories, was of eight days' duration. He earned steady promotion, rising rapidly from captain to lieutenant colonel; however he also attempted to resign from the army on several occasions and finally succeeded on grounds of ill health in 1779. Two years later he was practicing law in Albany, and his political career had begun.

Burr's rise to eminence was almost meteoric, especially after 1787. For reasons which have never been clear, he was not active in the events preceding and culminating in the constitutional convention, and his opinions relating to the Constitution are not even a matter of record. But in the period after ratification he became a foremost spokesman in New York of the anti-Federalist cause and the chief political antagonist of Alexander Hamilton. Hamilton, it is clear, disliked Burr from the first. Whether or not his hatred for Burr was, in Nathan Schachner's expression, "pathologic," it was obsessive, determined, and in the end, fatal to them both.

It is extremely difficult to account for Hamilton's intense animosity toward his fellow New Yorker. The two men were of widely different backgrounds, tastes, and abilities, but rivalry and difference does not account for Hamilton's self-expressed feeling that it was his "religious duty to oppose [Burr's] career." Burr reciprocated the dislike, but he did not reciprocate Hamilton's intense hatred; it is noteworthy that he gave Hamilton every opportunity to withdraw the charges that precipitated the duel. Hamilton's letters repeatedly refer to Burr as "unprincipled," "ambitious," "extravagant," "bold," "intriguing," and possessed of an "impeached integrity." "In a word," he declares in one letter, "if we have an embryo Caesar in the United States, 'tis Burr."

Burr's later career has the effect of making Hamilton seem prescient, but it was a career which Hamilton helped to shape. In setting out to destroy Frankenstein, Hamilton succeeded in creating him, and Frankensteinlike, the "monster" eventually turned on his creator. But it was not until that confrontation at Weehauken Bluff in 1804 that Hamilton had clear, compelling reasons to fear Burr.

The Burr who fired the fatal shot early in the morning of July 11, 1804, was vice-president of the United States and had previously served as a United States senator. He was considered one of the two most brilliant lawyers in the state of New York—the other was Hamilton—and, more than that, he had failed by only three votes to be chosen president by the House of Representatives in 1801. But in 1804, at the time of the duel, he had few friends, little influence, and dim political prospects. Hamilton had seen to the friends, the influence, and the prospects, and what he had left undone in life, he completed in death.

It is doubtful that Burr's career would have terminated so abruptly had Hamilton not waged his determined campaign against him. Burr's personal failings were varied, but his virtues and vices were no more unevenly balanced than those of his contemporaries. He was not above some exploitation of politics for personal gain, but such behavior was not uncommon among the public men of his day, including Hamilton. The long series of amours for which he became notorious did not begin, apparently, until some time after his wife's fatal illness in 1794. Moreover there is nothing to suggest, prior to the duel, that he was prey to a ruthless and unprincipled ambition. Although he required only three votes to be elected president by the

House of Representatives in 1801, through twenty-nine ballots over a period of seven days he made no effort to secure the necessary support. As one representative later wrote in a letter, "The means existed of electing Burr, but this required his cooperation. By deceiving one man (a great blockhead) and tempting two (not incorruptible), he might have secured a majority of the states." Burr did not choose to cooperate, but the point of the remark and of remarks similar in tone which were made to Hamilton was lost on Burr's archenemy.

It is tempting to provide an Actonian interpretation of Burr's later career, but his role in the so-called Burr conspiracy does not lend itself to that purpose. Burr's attempt to create an empire to the South, at the expense of Spain and Mexico, may have been ill-advised, but it would not have been stigmatized as "conspiracy" had not Jefferson shared something of Hamilton's obsession. The Burr expedition enjoyed considerable popularity, not least with Andrew Jackson, and it should be noted that Burr was acquitted of the charge of treason in a trial presided over by Chief Justice Marshall. It is also relevant that the failure of the "conspiracy" was not followed by other "conspiracies" or "plots."

It is difficult, therefore, to find evidence in Burr's life that "power tends to corrupt . . . ," or evidence, for that matter, that power*less-ness* corrupts. On the whole, Burr bore the multiple adversities of his life with cheerful courage and equanimity. Even the deaths in rapid succession of his beloved daughter (an only child) and grandchild did not provoke expressions of self-pity; he had long been resolved, as he put it, to "accept the inevitable without repining." So far as can be determined, he was without bitterness to the end, and with regard to Hamilton, without blame. "Had I read Sterne more than Voltaire," he remarked in his last years, with perhaps more charity than his old foe deserved, "I might have thought the world large enough for Hamilton and me."

PREDISPOSITIONS TOWARD POWER

We so far have established support for the hypotheses that power-seeking in and of itself does not engender corruption and that sudden increases and decreases of power are not invariably attended by corruption. But it may be argued that the careers of Arthur, Van Buren, and Burr are unique in American politics and constitute unique exceptions to the Acton rule. Certainly in the popular imagination the images conjured up by "power tends to corrupt . . ." have been typically those of the major political bosses who dominated local governments in the late nineteenth and early twentieth centuries. Men like Blaine, Tweed, Penrose, and Wood have long served as conventional objects of the Acton aphorism employed as epithet. There can be no question that many of these politicians were ruthless power-seekers and proven corruptionists. Were they also exemplars of the Acton principle?

Analysis of the careers of thirty of these politicians suggests that, broadly speaking, there have been two conspicuous types of political boss in the United States and that neither type lends itself to the Acton generality.[9] The typologies which follow are composite crea-

---

[9] The political bosses selected for analysis were: Albert A. Ames, Martin Behrman, James G. Blaine, Edward Butler, Roscoe Conkling, George B. Cox, Richard Croker, James M. Curley, Israel W. Durham, William Flynn, Frank Hague, John Kelly, Martin Lomasney, Frederick Lundin, Christopher Lyman Magee, Hugh McLaughlin, James McManes, Charles F. Murphy, George W. Olvany, Boies Penrose, Thomas C. Platt, George Washington Plunkitt, Matthew S. Quay, Abraham Reuf, Roger C. Sullivan, Timothy Sullivan, Samuel J. Tilden, William M. Tweed, Edwin H. Vare, and Fernando Wood. The standard work on the municipal bosses is Harold Zink, *City Bosses in the United States* (Durham, N.C.: Duke University Press, 1930). A large number of the individuals mentioned have never received detailed biographical treatment. Of those biographies and other books that deal at length with individual bosses the following are especially important. For Blaine: T. C. Crawford, *James G. Blaine* (Philadelphia: Edgewood Co., 1893); Mary A. Dodge, *Biography of James G. Blaine* (Norwich, Conn.: Henry Bill Publishing Co., 1895); David S. Muzzey, *James G. Blaine, A Political Idol of Other Days* (New York: Dodd, Mead & Co., 1934); Charles E. Russell, *Blaine of Maine* (New York: Holt, Rinehart & Winston, Inc., 1931). For Conkling: Alfred R. Conkling, *Life and Letters of Roscoe Conkling* (New York: C. L. Webster & Co., 1884); George C. Gorham, *Roscoe Conkling Vindicated*, Reprinted from *New York Herald*, June 4, 1888. Croker: Alfred H. Lewis, *Richard Croker* (New York: Life Publishing Co., 1901); Theodore L. Stoddard, *Master of Manhattan, The Life of Richard Croker* (New York: Longmans, Green & Co., Inc., 1949). For Curley: Wendell D. Howie, *The Reign of James the First* (Cambridge: Warren Publications, Inc., 1936); Joseph F. Dinneen, *The Purple Shamrock* (New York: W. W. Norton & Company, Inc., 1949). For Hague: Dayton McKean, *The Boss: The Hague Machine in Action* (Boston: Houghton Mifflin Company, 1940). For Penrose: Robert D. Bowden, *Boies Penrose: Symbol of An Era* (Philadelphia: Chilton Company, 1937). For Platt: his *Autobiography* (New York: McBride Books, 1910); Harold F. Gosnell, *Boss Platt and His New York Machine* (Chicago: University of Chicago Press, 1924). For Plunkitt: William L. Riordan, *Plunkitt of Tammany Hall* (New York: Alfred A. Knopf, Inc., 1948). For Reuf: Walton Bean, *Boss Reuf's San Francisco* (Berkeley: University of California

tions based on representative figures—the identifying characteristics of each type are not wholly those of any one individual—and we shall here distinguish them by the terms *game politician* and *gain politician.*

Our first type of boss, the *game politician,* was of early American stock and upper-class background. His father was important in business circles in the community and active in civic affairs. A Puritan in morals and a conservative in politics, the father had a strong sense of family position, and he impressed upon his son at an early age his own conviction that the best traditions of America, which the family represented, were being engulfed by a rising tide of immigration and radicalism. The father was also convinced that discipline produced moral virtue, and he was firm and unyielding in meting out punishment for youthful infractions. Since the home rules were rather strict, the boy was never certain when he was called to his father's study whether his father was to administer a sermon, a scolding, or both.

Timid, frail, and ill a good part of the time, the boy's mother played a relatively minor role in his life. Although she loved the boy (who was an only child) and longed to comfort him after an especially painful session in the study, she rarely interfered, knowing that any intercession from her was apt to increase her husband's wrath rather than reduce it. She was not passive by nature, but her role as wife had always been passive in accordance with her husband's wishes. There were few expressions of affection in the family circle, and the boy's mother, especially in her later years, became increasingly occupied with an intensely personal type of religion. It is probable that her various illnesses served as expressions of acute inner distress.

Looking back from a later vantage point, the *game politician* could not remember a time as a boy when he had been happy, and he often remarked that his life had really begun when he left home for

Press, 1952). For Tilden: John Bigelow, *The Life of Samuel J. Tilden* (New York: Harper & Row, Publishers, 1893). For Tweed: Denis T. Lynch, *"Boss" Tweed, The Story of a Grim Generation* (New York: Liveright Publishing Corporation, 1927). For Wood: Samuel A. Pleasants, *Fernando Wood of New York* (New York: Columbia University Press, 1948). Timothy Sullivan and Tweed, among others, enjoy some prominence in Gustavus Myers, *The History of Tammany Hall* (New York: Liveright Publishing Corporation, 1917). Blaine receives extensive treatment in Matthew Josephson, *The Politicos* (New York: Harcourt, Brace & World, Inc., 1938).

college. He was a student leader and led an active campus life at college; he also earned sufficiently good grades to be admitted to an eminent law school. Following graduation he became attached to a well-known law firm in his home city, but the practice of law was never his foremost interest. His legal work brought him into close contact with local politicians, and within a short time he was one of them.

By the time he was thirty the *game politician* had held a variety of posts in the local government and majority party, and by the age of forty he was serving in the state legislature. During his middle years he was firmly in control of the state party organization with the power to appoint, or influence the appointment of, mayors, governors, United States senators, and other public officials; frequently he himself held one or the other of these offices. At the national level he was influential in nominating the presidential candidates of his party, and he was active, on occasion, in promoting his own chances. Frequent charges of corruption and the occasional success of reform movements threatened his career only intermittently. For most of his forty years of active political life he exercised effective control or was "the power behind the scenes."

In the course of after-dinner speeches at political banquets he was apt to make reference to "the great game of politics," and for him this expression was no mere cliché. A man of independent means, he did not exploit politics primarily, if at all, for personal gain, although he was privy to innumerable "deals" which involved the buying and selling of political favors. He regarded the uses and abuses of money in politics as legitimate, and he was always willing to arrange matters, if at all possible, to promote the financial interests of friends.

For the *game politician* politics functioned as the principal mode of self-expression and self-realization. He enjoyed "the game" for the ego rewards it offered, which were chiefly power, prestige, adulation, and a sense of importance. The manipulation of men and events, in which he excelled, served less his convictions, which were few, than as an exercise in strategy, which he valued for its own sake. Viewing the outcome as always more important than the issue, he derived great satisfaction from political victories of large and small consequence, no matter how obtained.

It was often said of our *game politician* that "he had many acquaintances and few friends." In reality he had many associates—most of them political dependents—few acquaintances, and no friends. He permitted himself a number of physical pleasures, respectable or otherwise, and on these occasions several cronies were usually to be found in his company. But his confidences in them were confined to political topics, and his association with them was based on a reciprocal exchange of various services. His relations with his immediate family were not close; indeed his wife and children saw less of him during his active life than certain key individuals in his political organization. As a result he is remembered less by his family than by the state which he dominated for so many years. His grave in the family plot is unattended, but his statue stands in front of the state capitol building.

Between 1870 and 1920 the *game politician*—to whom we shall return shortly—shared the national stage with another type of political boss, whom we shall here style the *gain politician*. Unlike his confrere in politics the second composite figure was the eldest of six children of an impoverished Irish immigrant family. The boy's father, an amiable if ineffectual man, was a bricklayer, but his earnings were too meager to support the family. The boy left school and worked at a variety of low-paid industrial jobs even before his father's death; after his death, which occurred when the boy was twelve years of age, the full burden of the family fell on the boy and his mother.

The mother lavished on the family all the love and attention of which she was capable, and the boy was her special favorite. Long after the other children were in bed, she and the boy would sit at the kitchen table discussing family affairs and exchanging gossip of the neighborhood. She occasionally would reminisce about the Ireland of her youth, and she often expressed a desire to make a stylish return someday to the Irish village in which she had lived as a young girl (she was later to realize this dream several times over). The boy confided his own ambitions and plans, and it became his practice over the years never to make any important decision without consulting her.

He meanwhile was fighting his way to power in the neighborhood gang. In the process he became quite skilled in fighting with fist or club, and he later was to put these methods to practical use in the rough-and-tumble ward politics of his day. The gang specialized in disrupting the political rallies of the minority party in the area, and it eventually became the nucleus of his own political machine. His good looks, stature, and powerful physique—as a young man he was able to lift a barrel of beer to shoulder height—endowed him with a certain physical magnetism which was of benefit throughout his career.

While still an adolescent he was entrusted with various missions by the long-time political boss in his section of the city. He and the boss became rather friendly, and eventually, on his own authority, he was able to distribute minor political favors and small amounts of patronage. In a few years he had created a machine within a machine, and he was then capable of dealing with rivals for the boss's favor from a position of strength. When the boss died, he moved quickly to consolidate his power, and within a short period he established himself as the head of the organization.

By this time he was approaching thirty years of age and had married. He had long since learned to turn political favors to his own financial interest; and with the proceeds derived from politics he had become the owner of one retail store and part-owner of several others. He also invested in various services which the city government patronized, the operations of which he could influence in his own favor. Meanwhile his political advancement was rapid, although it was confined to local party posts and municipal offices. He served as councilman, city treasurer, and mayor, and for many years was especially popular in the role of the latter. As city treasurer he was able to extend his power in the party, and long before he was mayor, he had become the most powerful political boss in the city's history.

He had also become one of the wealthiest. His opponents believed—and correctly—that in the city no contract was let, no tax collected, no post filled, and no facility established without his extracting a commission. It was revealed after his death that he was worth considerably more than one million dollars and that he had lived in lavish circumstances for a number of years. While his children were still young, he moved his family to a large mansion in the most fashionable part of town, and he also established his mother in a comfortable home, which was staffed by several servants. All seven children, with the exception of one daughter, who became a nun, attended expensive colleges. It was his wife's custom, on shopping trips, to be accompanied by her liveried personal chauffeur.

The *gain politician*, unlike the first type of political boss we have considered, had only a minor interest in state and national politics. He twice declined to be nominated for any higher office than mayor, and while he insisted upon being consulted, especially with regard to patronage, by governors and senators, he was primarily concerned to maintain good relations with "higher-ups." He was consistently opposed to, as he put it, "rocking the boat," and he dealt wrathfully with occasional mavericks, bolters, and would-be reformers within the party. Placing enormous importance on loyalty to the organization, he prided himself on the fact that he had never deserted a party stalwart, no matter what his personal or political difficulties.

Although the *gain politician* was firmly attached to few principles, he thought of himself as a "friend of the people," and indeed in a sense he was. He put innumerable relatives and friends on the city payroll and befriended countless others with gifts or loans of money. Widows, orphans, derelicts, the sick, the unemployed, the aged, the struggling, and the fallen—all of them received a hearing from him or his lieutenants and almost all of them received some tangible help. He donated large amounts of money to churches and synagogues, schools, hospitals, and orphanages and found time to sit at sickbeds and attend funerals. Radiating warmth, fellowship, and generosity, he earned a citywide personal following that was sufficiently large and loyal to maintain him in power through several damaging investigations of his political machine.

His marriage was a happy one, and no breath of domestic scandal touched him during his entire career. He derived much satisfaction from the achievements of his children, almost all of whom were successfully established in a business or profession at the time of his death. He also had a number of close personal friends, in whom he was in the habit of confiding his innermost thoughts. Several of these friends have written eulogistic biographies of his life; others have named their children after him. And for many citizens in the city he remains, many years after his death, a vital, almost living figure.

It is common to treat the *game politician* and *gain politician* not as cousins and not even as brothers in corruption, but as identical twins. The case histories, however, suggest that the term "corrupt boss" covers a multitude of sinners whose relations to each other are limited to a common involvement in political *flagrante delicto*. The fact of corruption may constitute only the weakest link between personality types as distinct from political careers. Moreover in the cases examined here, of which the *game* and *gain politicians* serve as archetypes, the variety of motivations is as diverse as the variety of acts.

Although psychological detail in the relevant biographical materials is, on the whole, sparse, the available data indicate that severe deprivation in early life is a key factor in the background of the corrupt boss. But it is the character of the deprivation, rather than deprivation as such, which is crucial for future behavior. Our *game politician*, for example, was deprived of love and emotional security during his formative years. It is clear that the cold and withdrawn personality of his later years was essentially developed in childhood as a protective response to a punitive environment. His inability as an adult to initiate and sustain close relations with family or friends is another derivative of the early period.

But a hostile environment may be made friendly and safe through manipulation, and we may infer that manipulative skills of various types were brought into play during the frequent sessions in the father's study. The study "game"—his boast in later life was that he was often able to "get around" his father on such occasions—was the early form of the political "game," and the deviousness, evasiveness, and capacity for intrigue of the mature politician also described the behavior pattern of the boy. In other essentials of personality development, however, the boy did not succeed in "getting around" his father. His repressed hatred of his father generated in adult life an hostility to others which created unnecessary difficulties in his political relationships. It is also true that his convictions were dominated by the rigid and outmoded conservative views with which he had been indoctrinated as a child. Although he was careful to avoid taking positions, he was generally understood to favor principles rather similar to those which had been espoused by his father. His arrogance and superciliousness, which were also qualities shared with his father, were added handicaps to his ambition for political preferment beyond the state level.

Unlike his father, however, the *game politician* was never attached to moral virtue, family honor, or a conscious, if misdirected, sense of tradition. His principal attachment was to the political "game" as such, to which all other considerations related as mere expedients. Self-realization and political realization were simple equivalents; indeed the personality system did not function well outside the political arena. But the stakes of the "game" were not confined to power as such. The demands of the self upon the environment largely related to deference values, and as Table I indicates, the "game" indulged a number of demands which had been blocked or frustrated elsewhere.

Table I

Personality System

Deprivation	Demand	Indulgence
Parental acceptance	Power	Office, bossism
Parental recognition	Respect	Votes, elections
Parental approval	Rectitude	Self-righteousness, moral superiority
Parental love	Affection	Following, clique, cronies

The major point, however, is that politics afforded our *game politician* a control of environment which facilitated the indulgence of demands. Relative to other arenas (home, business, profession) the political world was more indulgent of demands of the self upon the environment, and it also was capable of providing a greater variety of indulgences.

Viewed from this perspective, corruption was less an indulgence than a method by which the *game politician* maintained the necessary control of environment. While corruption served the end of power, power itself mainly functioned as the means of enforcing demands generated throughout the entire personality system. Put another way, power *and* corruption were the agencies by which the personality system sought to establish and support itself. The political man represented by the *game politician* was merely on older and more successful version of the emotionally deprived and rejected child.

For the *gain politician*, on the other hand, power and corruption were also functional, but functional in a different context of demands.

The early environment, except in its material aspect, was largely indulgent, and throughout his life he was supported by various emotionally satisfying relationships. His ambitions for office never extended beyond the local level, despite opportunities afforded to play a major role in state and national politics. Although he could be ruthless in dealing with opponents, his personal success owed much more to a genial disposition and warm manner than to coercive tactics. Although he consistently exploited politics for gain, it was a fact of his long career that he had won over many political enemies and never lost a friend.

The character of early deprivation largely related to the welfare values of well-being, wealth, skill, and enlightenment. But the demands of the self upon the environment, which were generated by such deprivation, were of a different order from those which developed in the personality system of the *game politician*. To begin with, the "self" was an aggregate rather than a single entity, a "we" rather than an "I." It initially included his mother, brothers, and sisters, and it later incorporated his wife and children. In a sense the collective self also embraced distant relatives, friends, and associates, because they too were beneficiaries of corrupt acts. In the second place, the demands of the self upon the environment were mainly confined to the wealth value; although other welfare values were important, the control of environment largely was exploited for material advantage. Finally the demands which were indulged, unlike demands related to deference values, rarely involved or affected interpersonal relations. Our *gain politician* did not need to dominate others; nor did he require their psychological submission. Indeed his success as a corruptionist owed much to the fact that he was never arrogant in his relations with peers or subordinates. In cheating the business leaders and taxpayers of their money, he was careful to avoid cheating them of their self-esteem.

It is also important that the *gain politician* was less cynical than indifferent to rectitude standards. Such standards had been absent in his early political training, and youthful experience had favored the view that politics essentially was a variety or form of commercial enterprise. In the context of prevailing political morality he would have considered it foolish *not* to exploit politics for gain and irresponsible to retire poor from office.

But the significant fact is that the *gain politician* employed corruption not in behalf of power, but in behalf of welfare values. As Table II illustrates, the political arena was indulgent of demands of the self upon the environment which related to early deprivation.

TABLE II

Personality System

Deprivation	Demand	Indulgence
Comfort	Well-being	"Rich" living
Income	Wealth	"Pay-offs," graft, "commissions"
Opportunity	Skill	"Deals," manipulations, promotions, combinations
Education	Enlightenment	"Inside" information, foreknowledge, "tips"

Again, as in the case of the *game politician,* power *and* corruption were directed toward specific ends which were generated in the personality system.

The analysis of composite "boss" types, therefore, does not support the Acton formula that "power tends to corrupt. . . ." The biographical test in general suggests, on the contrary, that corruption is a function of the relations among a number of variables in the personality system. The propositional form of such relations may be stated as follows:

1. Corruption may ensue when the early environment of the personality system promotes severe deprivation.
2. A background of severe deprivation may encourage the use of power in corrupt forms as a means of acquiring and maintaining environmental control.
3. The character of the early deprivation affects the purposes for which power is employed.
4. If the deprivation has been experienced mainly with reference to deference values, power in corrupt form will be employed in behalf of self-aggrandizement (*game politician*).
5. If the deprivation has been experienced mainly with reference to welfare values, power in corrupt form will be employed in behalf of material advantage (*gain politician*).
6. Power in and of itself neither expresses nor promotes any tendency, whether to corrupt or to ennoble.

These propositions, however, do not relate to the institutional settings in which power and corruption function and by which they may be affected. We now turn to this context to determine its relevance to the major problem.

The Institutional Test

Does the Acton formula also assert or imply a tendency with respect to institutional power? As has been noted, Acton believed that power had corrupted the papacy of the late Middle Ages. Although he never argued that institutions *per se* were prone to use power for corrupt purposes, Acton clearly believed that the men who presided over institutions—the "men in authority," to use his own phrase—were apt to exercise their power for corrupt ends. But although his distrust of power elites, especially those affecting an air of sanctimony and piety, was profound, Acton never explored the relationship between institutions and corruption. He was certain that the later mediaeval popes had been corrupted by power, but the question *why* the papacy had been corrupt during the thirteenth and fourteenth centuries seems to have eluded his inquiry. Nor is it enough to conclude that Acton, as a contemporary Catholic critic expressed it, had "Inquisition on the brain."

In focusing on the institutional context of "power tends to corrupt . . . ," it is apparent that institutions provide arenas in which power is sought, exercised, and abused. Power-seekers, in general, are drawn to those institutions which exemplify power or which afford scope for the expression of power. Indeed institutions may be transformed by individuals whose power-seeking is reflected in institutional growth and expansion; thus the papacy of the Middle Ages, the Supreme Court of the early nineteenth century, and the German General Staff in the period before World War I. But institutional power in the broadest sense is not necessarily a consequence of the power urge of individuals. The dominance of X corporation in its particular field of enterprise may owe a good deal to the personality of Y, its long-time chairman of the board; the dominance of the modern corporation in economic life derives from the nature of modern industrial society. Although there can be no doubt that the expansion in modern times of presidential power owes something to the personalities of recent chief executives, notably the two Roosevelts and Wilson, it remains true that executive authority everywhere in the world has enormously increased during the past thirty years. The authority wielded by the American president, the British prime minister, the French president, and the German chancellor far surpasses that exercised by their predecessors of a generation ago.

Examining American political institutions in the light of the Acton aphorism, one is almost led to conclude that the relationship between institutional power and corruption is inverse. Corrupt practices were rife during the administrations of two of the *weaker* presidents, Grant and Harding. The decline in importance of the House of Representatives after the Civil War was accompanied by a remarkable increase in the number of corrupt acts engaged in by House members; between 1863 and 1883 every speaker of the House in office a full term or more was charged with corruption. There was relatively little corruption in state assemblies before 1850, when the assemblies were extremely powerful organs of state government; with the eclipse of the assemblies after 1850 corruption increased.

These examples, of course, do not establish an inverse relationship between power and corruption, but they do suggest that the relationship is far more complex than the Acton formula would indicate. If "power tends to corrupt . . . ," how can one account for the fact that no president and no justice of the Supreme Court has ever been charged with, much less convicted of, corruption in office? And if power does *not* corrupt, how can one account for widespread institutionalized corruption at particular times? To answer such questions, however tentatively, one must deal with institutional contexts and, in particular, account for the alternating periods of rectitude and corruption that have characterized the histories of a number of institutions.

As noted earlier, the presidency, as distinct from the executive branch, has always been free of the taint of corruption. Although every presidential administration has included officials whose political services were available at a price, the evidence does not suggest that corruption has been a conspicuous feature of executive branch behavior from 1789 to 1960. Most historians would agree, however, that the Grant and Harding administrations were characterized by the relative absence of rectitude standards on the part of high-ranking political personages. Corruption in the Grant administration involved, among others, the secretary of war, a number of treasury officials, two vice-presidents, and two speakers of the House. The so-called "Whisky Rings" made use of Grant's private secretary, and it will be recalled that Jim Fisk and Jay Gould worked through Grant's brother-in-law in their efforts to corner the gold market. Corruption during the Harding years implicated the attorney general, the secretary of interior, the secretary of the navy, the director of the veterans bureau, and the alien property custodian.

It is conventional to account for the corruption of the Grant and Harding eras by reference to the low ethical and moral standards that obtained in general throughout American society after the Civil War and during the 1920's. Certainly such corruption owed something to the unbridled materialism and frenzied quest for gain that typified public manners and tastes—to the spirit, in the words of Vernon L. Parrington, of "The Great Barbecue." No doubt, too, corruption owed something to the toughminded political "realism" of the empire-builders and magnates who did not hesitate to exploit legislatures and courts for their own private ends. "If you have to pay money to have the right thing done," Colis P. Huntington of the Southern Pacific wrote a political agent,

> it is only just and fair to do it . . . If a man has the power to do great evil and won't do right unless he is bribed to do it, I think the time spent will be gained when it is a man's duty to go up and bribe the judge. A man that will cry out against them himself will also do these things himself . . .[10]

In the six years between 1866 and 1872, according to Richard Hofstadter, "the Union Pacific spent $400,000 on bribes; between 1875 and 1885 graft cost the Central Pacific as much as $500,000 annually. Little wonder that an honest Republican of the old school like Walter Q. Gresham could describe his party as 'an infernally corrupt concern,' or that Senator Grimes of Iowa . . . could say in 1870: 'I believe it is today the most corrupt and debauched political party that ever existed.' 'One might search the whole list of Congress, Judiciary,

---

[10] Quoted in Richard Hofstadter, *The American Political Tradition and the Men Who Made It* (New York: Alfred A. Knopf, Inc., 1948), p. 163.

and Executive during the twenty-five years 1870-1895,' concluded
Henry Adams, 'and find little but damaged reputation.' " [11]

Adams may have exaggerated, but he was neither the first nor
the last observer to see clearly that political ethics enjoyed an intimate
relationship with business ethics. "On the national level," Senator
Paul H. Douglas has more recently written,

> there can be little doubt where the initiative lies. In most cases, the
> pressure comes from private sources which are seeking to influence or
> control government. In the main, they are the enticers and the entrap-
> pers, while the government officials who consent are commonly the
> enticed and entrapped. Some officials may yield willingly or without
> much resistance, but they seldom begin the liaison.[12]

It is also true that a public conditioned to expect political corruption
is much more tolerant of the delinquent businessman than the erring
civil servant. Exposure of the former is seldom attended by public
outrage and insistence that he seek another means of livelihood.[13]
Exposure of the latter, on the other hand, is almost always followed
by demands that he resign or be forced from public office.

But under what conditions, in Douglas' words, do political officials "yield willingly or without much resistance"? Examination of
institutions supports the hypothesis that the tendency toward rectitude or corruption at a given time relates to the prestige and morale
of the institution under examination. We would argue, further:

1. If the leadership of the institution does not serve as a rectitude
   model, those belonging to or serving in the institution may "yield
   willingly or without much resistance."
2. If the membership of an institution does not collectively enforce
   rectitude standards, the tendency toward individual corruption is
   increased.
3. Institutions of high and increasing prestige and morale are more
   likely to attract ambitious men concerned with furthering their

---

[11] Hofstadter, *American Political Tradition and the Men Who Made It*, p.
168.

[12] Paul H. Douglas, *Ethics in Government* (Cambridge: Harvard University
Press, 1952), pp. 24-25. See also George A. Graham, *Morality in American
Politics* (New York: Random House, 1952).

[13] The relative tolerance accorded unethical behavior in business is docu-
mented in Edwin H. Sutherland, *White Collar Crime* (New York: Holt, Rinehart & Winston, Inc., 1949).

careers than corrupt men interested in promoting their personal fortunes.

4. Institutions declining in power or prestige are more likely to attract corrupt men interested in promoting their personal fortunes than ambitious men concerned with furthering their careers.

The histories of the federal executive, legislative, and judicial branches lend abundant support to these hypotheses. The presidency itself has enjoyed immense power and prestige from the beginning, and this fact is important in understanding the utter incorruptibility of the American chief executive. But although no president has been corrupt, several have exercised weak and timorous leadership or have demonstrated a marked indifference to rectitude standards in their appointments to public office. In all such cases of which we have knowledge, there have been significant examples of corrupt behavior on the part of department, bureau, and agency officials. There has been less corruption, on the other hand, in those administrations that have enforced standards of probity and honesty from the top down. Within the executive branch, patterns of rectitude and corruption are related to prestige, morale, and power. New administrations, especially those of a reformist nature, have generally attracted men ambitious for their careers and reputations. Eager to identify themselves with new programs and policies, such men and the agencies to which they have been attached have exemplified, as a rule, the highest rectitude standards. In the initial years of power a conscious moral tone and a dedicated enthusiasm pervades the entire area of government. And even those who do not share the prevailing mood are affected by the knowledge that corrupt acts, if exposed, are not likely to be tolerated, much less condoned.

High moral dedication, however, like other characteristics of administration, may gradually yield to apathy and complacency. There is a "natural tendency," writes one experienced participant in government,

> for the quality of administration to degenerate with time. When the people decide that the Government should take on some new function and Congress sets up an agency to administer it, enthusiasm runs high . . . But soon ossification and degeneration set in. The early enthusiasts die off or leave Government service. Some remain but lose most of their fire and zeal. The public thinks the battle has been won

and turns its attention to other things . . . in a short time an agency which was originally alert and public-spirited becomes waterlogged, indolent, and corrupt.[14]

Low salaries paid to officials, the frustrations of office, the increasing pressures brought upon policy decisions—these and other negative factors may take their toll of efficiency and competence, if not of rectitude. In a recent study of the independent regulatory commissions Marver Bernstein has argued persuasively that a "life cycle" is characteristic of such agencies. In the early years of the commissions the policy-making and administrative processes are carried through with vigor and imagination. Although political considerations in making appointments are not without importance,

> it is not uncommon for new agencies to start with carefully selected and admirably qualified personnel. But as an agency's pioneering period passes, and it becomes accepted as part of the governmental establishment, the incentive to make outstanding appointments dwindles, and the way opens for political considerations to claim a large part.[15]

The long tenures of most commissioners attached to the Interstate Commerce Commission and Federal Trade Commission, Bernstein comments, have led not to continuity and stability, but to inertia and paralysis.

Analyzing the legislative arena, one is tempted to account for rectitude or corruption solely in terms of the increasing or decreasing prestige of the legislative branch. It is clear, for example, that the "damaged reputation" noted by Henry Adams coincided with a sharp decline in the prestige of both houses of Congress. Although there was some corruption in the Senate and House during the years preceding the Civil War, it was political ambition rather than opportunities for corruption that attracted most men to legislative careers. Indeed,

---

[14] Paul H. Douglas in *The New York Times Magazine*, April 1, 1951, quoted in "Establishment of a Commission on Ethics in Government," *Hearings before a Subcommittee to Study Senate Concurrent Resolution 21 of the Committee on Labor and Public Welfare*, United States Senate, Eighty-second Congress, First Session, June and July 1951, pp. 558-559.

[15] Quoted from *Board of Investigation and Research, Practices and Procedures of Governmental Control*, House Document No. 678 (1944), Seventy-eighth Congress, Second Session, p. 27, in Marver Bernstein, *Regulating Business by Independent Commission* (Princeton: Princeton University Press, 1955), pp. 106-107.

the prestige of the House of Representatives was such as to make a number of congressmen, notably Henry Clay, reluctant to leave the House for a seat in the Senate. Membership in the House, and especially the speakership, were regarded as providing more certain access than a Senate seat to higher positions in the government, including the presidency.[16] During the era that closed with the Civil War three speakers of the House were nominated for the presidency, and one of them, James K. Polk, was subsequently elected president.[17] In the one hundred years since the election of Abraham Lincoln only one speaker, James G. Blaine, has been nominated—unsuccessfully— for the highest office.[18]

The declining prestige of Congress after the Civil War, however, provides only one part of the explanation for the prevalence of legislative corruption in the so-called "Gilded Age." In the House of Representatives, especially, corrupt behavior owes a good deal to the failure of both the leadership and membership to enforce rectitude standards. Although the leaders of the Senate and the House after the Civil War were not, for the most part, less able or capable than their pre-War predecessors, unlike them they were largely passive in the face of widespread evidence that much legislative business was transacted in a corrupt fashion. Moreover, an indifferent attitude toward corrupt behavior of members remains characteristic of both houses. As George A. Graham has observed, the Senate and House have taken disciplinary action "chiefly when issues have been forced upon them by publicity or other outside pressure, and punishment has been meager." No senator or congressman "has been expelled or disciplined in any way for receiving money, gifts, services, swimming pools, lakes, or anything else from contractors doing business with the government."

---

[16] The history of the speakership has been treated extensively in Mary Parker Follett, *The Speaker of the House of Representatives* (New York: Longmans, Green & Co., Inc., 1896); Hubert Bruce Fuller, *The Speakers of the House* (Boston: Little, Brown & Co., 1909); and Chang-Wei Chiu, *The Speaker of the House of Representatives since 1896* (New York: Columbia University Press, 1928).

[17] It is also worth noting that John Quincy Adams, after he ceased to be president, did not regard a seat in the House of Representatives as beneath his dignity.

[18] It is proper to mention, however, that John Garner, speaker of the House from 1931-33, served as vice-president from 1933-41.

In fact, according to Graham, "no member has been expelled for violation of the law even when indicted, tried, and convicted of crime." The "implication" of such inaction "is that according to Congressional standards anything goes, not only everything the law allows, but also what it does not allow." [19] Unable or unwilling to enforce rectitude standards with regard to its own membership, the legislative branch is hardly in a position to establish itself as a moral model for behavior at executive and administrative levels.

In the annals of governmental history the Supreme Court alone enjoys an unsullied reputation for honesty and incorruptibility. The justices of the Supreme Court, unlike a number of the judges of the lower federal courts and state courts, have been men of unimpeachable integrity. Although political considerations have had an important influence on the appointment (and confirmation) of justices, and the Court has often been accused of partisanship and bias in decision-making,[20] it has never been suggested, much less proven, that a Supreme Court justice could be "bought" or bribed. There is no evidence, in short, that any of the justices who sat on the Court from 1789-1960 benefited personally from decisions promoting the interests of business, labor, agriculture, or other sections of American society.

The integrity of the Supreme Court, like that of the presidency, owes much to the fact that the Court, almost from the beginning, has enjoyed immense power and prestige. No justice has ever regarded membership of the highest tribunal as providing opportunity for personal gain, and most have viewed their appointments to the Court as capstones of careers in law and politics. Although the larger number of justices have not been men of the utmost distinction, it remains true, in the words of one student of the subject, that the majority "were individuals of more than average ability and legal training who

---

[19] Graham, *Morality in American Politics*, p. 93. "These standards of discipline," he continues, "are not the characteristics of a body that has a high morale, is confident of its mission, and proud of its integrity . . . the trend of behavior points to the conclusion that Congress lacks the morale to defend its own integrity." For case studies of congressional corruption see H. H. Wilson, *Congress: Corruption and Compromise* (New York: Holt, Rinehart & Winston, Inc., 1951).

[20] An analysis of these charges is presented in a forthcoming study of Supreme Court controversies by Paul Tillett.

conscientiously fulfilled their duties with vigor and high intelligence." [21] And in virtually every period of our history the Court has included "great" justices, men who possessed outstanding intellectual and personal qualities—such justices as "Marshall, William Johnson, Taney, Curtis, Campbell, Miller, Field, Bradley, Holmes, Hughes, Stone, Brandeis, and Cardozo. . . ." [22] The "great" justices have not been distinguished merely for legal scholarship or the exercise of judicial statesmanship. They have also exemplified the highest rectitude standards. If, as a consequence, the Court has served as "the keeper of the American conscience"—whether conscience be defined broadly as our political and social conscience or, more narrowly, as that "of the American upper-middle class"—[23] it has also served as the keeper of our moral and ethical conscience; in a word, as the symbol of rectitude in our national life.

Is it coincidence, in terms of our analysis, that the institutions of the presidency and the Supreme Court have symbolic significance for the nation and that Congress does not? We would argue that the symbolic roles of the president and Supreme Court justices are essential to an understanding of the institutional context of rectitude/corruption. From the time of Washington and Marshall it has been expected that presidents and justices should be, like Caesar's wife and the British royal family, "above suspicion." *Game politicians* they may have been, or political careerists, or opportunists of the most obvious type. Their early careers may not stand much scrutiny or may support serious doubts as to their qualifications for higher office. But once they reach the White House or the Supreme Court, they are expected to be, and with few exceptions have been, beyond moral reproach. The president, as the spokesman for our best traditions and aspirations, and the justices, as the collective symbol of the supreme law of the Constitution, have been forced by role and position to uphold the highest ethical standards. *Gain politicians,* for this reason, must pursue careers elsewhere in the government, and it is apparent that their activities have largely been confined to those areas of govern-

---

[21] John R. Schmidhauser, *The Supreme Court: Its Politics, Personalities, and Procedures* (New York: Holt, Rinehart & Winston, Inc., 1960), p. 154.

[22] Schmidhauser, *The Supreme Court: Its Politics, Personalities, and Procedures,* p. 194.

[23] Schmidhauser, *The Supreme Court: Its Politics, Personalities, and Procedures,* p. 59.

ment that possess little or no rectitude tradition or symbolic significance: state legislatures, city halls, the inferior courts, Congress, and
the administrative departments and agencies of the national government.

In sum, in assessing tendencies toward rectitude or corruption,
the institutional test is an important adjunct to biographical analysis.
Although we can do no more than make a beginning in such an assessment, it is abundantly clear that the Acton formula is both too
simple and too generalized to describe, much less explain, the contexts in which corruption or rectitude result. We now turn to certain
further applications of our findings and to additional research areas
that, in the future, will require extended investigation.

Chapter Three

The Emerging Power Situation

Rectitude does not vary with power. Power does not necessarily lead to corruption or to ennoblement. The connection between rectitude and power depends upon context, upon various factor-combinations in personality and society. Our inquiry has established a substantial basis in fact for the proposition that the method of thinking that found expression in Lord Acton's aphorism is fundamentally invalid. It lacks contextuality.

Must we conclude that the answer to the question of how power affects rectitude is that "sometimes it does; sometimes it doesn't"? Definitely not. The intellectual challenge is to devise procedures by which the specific combinations responsible for the fluctuations of power and rectitude in concrete circumstances can be identified. These combinations account for trend; they are helpful in projecting the course of future events. If we postulate an overriding goal of policy, such as the reduction or elimination of corruption, we may be able to devise the alternatives of policy most likely to succeed.

A fivefold problem-solving approach is implied: What outcomes are sought? What trends to date realize or fail to realize the goal? What factor-patterns condition the degree of realization? If we assume that we have no influence over the future, what is the probability that goals will in fact be achieved? If we assume that policies can be affected, what policies, if adopted, will expedite desired results?

65

These questions, concisely summarized, refer to goal, trend, condition, projection, and alternative.

It is not necessary to argue in general terms about goal. Only a whimsical use of words can justify the proclamation of corruptness as a goal of the American commonwealth. Specific interpretations may differ; and serious thinkers may make a convincing argument in favor of resort to corrupt practice in particular circumstances. But corruption is a negative symbol; more than that, it is a negative concept.

The critical part of our present enterprise has been accomplished. Before concluding the study, however, we desire to move in a more positive direction and to propose some provisional implications that suggest themselves when we make an affirmative, though partial, application of the contextual approach to the consideration of power and rectitude in the United States.

More particularly this calls for a highly generalized preliminary model of the factor-combinations that affect the impact of power upon corruption and correctness. It is not within the scope of the present study to more than indicate how this general model may eventually be adapted to account for the fluctuating trends in corruption that have appeared in the history of the American commonwealth.

A further task—one of obvious pertinence to the future of public order—is the projection of coming developments in the role of corruption and power. We shall glance at the total configuration of American life and select features of the social process that are likely to affect, or to be affected by, the sequence of future events.

We do not leave it at that: our method calls for more, even in these limited and mainly illustrative exercises. Can we point to policy moves, conducted by appropriate strategies, which if attempted would influence the course of future development and narrow the gap between aspiration and performance?

Throughout these pages it will be manifest that the tools of thought required by a problem-solving, contextual method are intimately and continuously interrelated. By moving among standpoints and procedures we clarify the whole. To estimate or affect the future it is necessary to reinspect past trends and conditioning factors. The clarification of goal takes into account contingencies in the past and future.

Power and Rectitude in a System
of Public Order: A General Model

By the American system of public order we refer to the basic pattern of value distribution and the fundamental institutions that receive protection from the legal system. The legal system is part of the whole.[1]

Since the proclaimed norms of a system of public order are often disregarded in everyday life, it is essential to distinguish between the established doctrine of a legal, political, and social system and the degree of harmony between authority and control that constitutes the public order as we understand the term. In the American legal system many acts are stigmatized as corrupt, and sanctions are laid down for the presumably small percentage of deviations from the norm. As everyone knows, however, sanctions often are not applied to conduct that deviates from an articulated norm. Many times, too, prescriptions laid down in a statute book—conventionally assumed to be authoritative—contradict norms that are widely accepted as ethically obligatory. Gambling provides flagrant examples. In many jurisdictions no attempt is made to apply statutory prohibitions of gambling, since the activities that come within the nominal scope of the prohibition are part of the accepted moral order. (The statute, perhaps, is a carry-over from earlier days that no one has bothered to erase.)

As students of law and politics—conceiving law as the authoritative *and* controlling component of power—we are concerned with the "realities" as well as the "formalities" of a political system. Our professional responsibility is to confront *conventional* images of what is supposed to be true with *functional* images—established by appropriate research—depicting what in fact is so.[2]

---

[1] For research and analysis dealing with public order see, for example, M. S. McDougal and associates, *Public Order of the World Community* (New Haven: Yale University Press, 1960); G. H. Dession, *Law, Administration and Public Order* (Charlottesville, Va.: Michie Co., 1948); G. H. Dession, "The Technique of Public Order: Evolving Concepts of Criminal Law," *Buffalo Law Review* (1955); G. H. Dession and H. D. Lasswell, "Public Order Under Law: The Role of the Advisor-Draftsman in the Formation of Code and Constitution," *Yale Law Journal*, **65** (1955), 174-175.

[2] A step in this direction is R. Arens and H. D. Lasswell, *In Defense of Public Order, The Emerging Field of Sanction Law* (New York: Columbia University Press, 1961).

The system of public order in fact is our concern. When, for example, we examine corruption in the political and legal system of a commonwealth, we must recognize that some degree of corruption is sufficiently stable to be included as part of the actual system. The act of proclaiming stringent norms of rectitude is itself part of the established order; so too is disregard for many proclaimed norms in whole or in part (at national, state, or local levels). Since the effective, as distinct from the formal, constitution of a body politic is composed of the relatively stable patterns that occur within it, we must remember that degrees of corruption are part of the effective constitution of the United States, which—need it be said again?—is not to be confounded with words inscribed upon a particular piece of parchment. The constitution of the American commonwealth is reaffirmed every day whenever any established expectation or norm is adhered to; it is amended daily as new patterns gain credence on the basis of actual conduct. The conventional organs of government—federal, state, or local—are embedded in the social process; they are not, however, necessarily decisive in shaping prescriptive norms or in maintaining an effective expectation that severe deprivations will be directed at deviants.

These broad considerations are indispensable to the candid study of a phenomenon so pervasive and significant as corruption. We begin by outlining a generalized model of rectitude and power by imagining a Utopia in which corruption does not exist. Such a model provides the greatest possible visibility to the imperfections found in concrete circumstances.

The most inclusive "empty" generalization, which merely reiterates the maximization postulate,[3] is that society is without corruption when its members expect to be better off by acting correctly than corruptly and are capable of perceiving and living up to the appropriate norms. This proposition is far from empty when some of its

---

[3] The maximization postulate can be given relatively stringent or permissive interpretation as the circumstances of a problem dictate. For a permissive version see H. Simon, "Some Strategic Considerations in the Construction of Social Science Models," in P. F. Lazarsfeld, ed., *Mathematical Thinking in the Social Sciences* (Glencoe, Ill.: Free Press of Glencoe, Inc., 1954), chap. 8. As a rule economists have used more restrictive interpretations; see J. von Neumann and O. Morgenstern, *Theory of Games and Economic Behavior* (Princeton: Princeton University Press, 1947).

formidable implications are sketched. In a corruption-free system the socialization process modifies predispositions in such a way that by the time a new generation enters adult life, the following propositions are true of each individual: he is identified with the whole community; he expects to be better off by conforming to the norms of the community than by violating them; he demands of himself that he conform to the norms of the society; and he has the capabilities required to perceive and adhere to the common myth. Furthermore the interactions that occur in adult life continue to provide net advantages and capabilities to those who conform.[4]

We can enrich the working model to be used in investigating any particular body politic by modifying the corruption-free image in ways that systematically highlight significant features of the actual situation. Taking a lead from Plato's analysis of character and constitution,[5] we may begin with changes in the routines of adult-to-adult relationships; then we may explore the consequences as they spread to adult-to-child and hence to child-to-child relationships. Assume that adult evaluations of the importance of rectitude, wealth, and other value outcomes change. The process is accompanied by some confusion and conflict in applying older norms of conduct to concrete situations. The resulting discrepancies between conduct and the proclaimed prescriptions of public order influence the socialization process by providing a confused and often contradictory set of patterns for the rising generation to incorporate within their personality systems.

Such a generalized picture is relevant to the history of the American commonwealth. The original colonists attached high importance to rectitude, which they expressed in religious worship and in the

<hr>

[4] Studies of political socialization include H. E. Hyman, *Political Socialization* (Glencoe, Ill.: Free Press of Glencoe, Inc., 1959); R. E. Lane, *Political Life; Why People Get Involved in Politics* (Glencoe, Ill.: Free Press of Glencoe, Inc., 1959); D. Easton and R. D. Hess, "Youth and the Political System," S. M. Lipset and L. Lowenthal, *Culture and Social Character; The Work of David Riesman Reviewed* (Glencoe, Ill.: Free Press of Glencoe, Inc., 1961), pp. 226-251.

[5] See H. D. Lasswell, "Political Constitution and Character," *Psychoanalysis and the Psychoanalytic Review*, **46** (1960), 3-18; also "Democratic Character," *Political Writings of H. D. Lasswell* (Glencoe, Ill.: Free Press of Glencoe, Inc., 1951); H. D. Lasswell, *Power and Personality* (New York: W. W. Norton & Company, Inc., 1948).

subordination of conduct in all realms to the presumed requirements of divine will. The colonists soon found themselves in conflict as a result of the growing importance assigned to such a secular value as wealth. As usual when value perspectives are rearranged, the process was by no means fully conscious and was accompanied by controversy over the application of established prescriptions to specific circumstances. As a rule controversy did not take the form of flatly rejecting traditional norms in regard to work on Sunday or sumptuary restrictions. Since traditional homage was paid to morals and religion, the debate was often in terms of concession to "necessity," such as preventing the enrichment of the ungodly to the detriment of the saints.

As the gap widened between proclaimed norms and adult behavior, the socialization process in America was affected by determined attempts of clergymen and teachers to restore the earlier equilibrium by indoctrinating the young. The result was to intensify the general state of confusion and conflict regarding rectitude and to contribute to corruption as well as correctness in American life. Corruption arose as young people found themselves penalized if they tried to live up to proclaimed norms when they competed with less scrupulous merchants, manufacturers, bankers, journalists, lawyers, and politicians.

It is commonly said that corruption varies directly with the speed of change and hence that the essential explanation of discrepancies between articulate norm and overt behavior is change. An assertion that "change is the enemy of norm" has the plausibility of the Acton principle that "power tends to corrupt . . . "; and it is subject to the same limitations. It is also true that "change is the mother of norm"; novel circumstances create demands to resolve confusion and contradiction by respecifying ancient prescriptions or by articulating new standards. It is also possible to defend the assertion that "absence of change brings the attrition of norm," such as when ancient norms become empty rituals whose original aim and role are forgotten. The significant question is: Under what conditions does change foster corruption or rectitude?

A critical question has been implied above: When does *confusion* result from changing perspectives of value outcome? When does confusion occur? The answer: When *lapses of time* allow confusion to continue and permit corrupt practices to take root. More explicitly:

sets of expectations arise that take some degree of corruptness for granted; *vested interests* are built into the new situation and militate against consensus upon norms of the common good. Lapses of time occur *when immediate steps are not taken* to employ collective processes to promptly clarify confusion. In our smoothly functioning Utopian model the "equipment of norms" is presumed to be specified so definitely in each situation that each individual, old or young, understands what conduct is appropriate (or immediately demands and abides by clarification). In short the intelligence and appraisal phases of the decision process operate without delay to clarify prescription by elucidating both contingency and normative statements regarding conduct. Unawareness of change is overcome by alert intelligence and appraisal activity; and predispositions to misperceive are kept weak by the techniques employed in the socialization process.

In the American commonwealth lapses of time are often permitted to intervene between events that precipitate confusion or contradiction and the act of adjusting a prescription. When microchanges are involved, the process may at first attract little enlightened attention. If innovations are tiny, the issue may not seem worth pressing to a determination; in the end a subtle accumulation of corrupt practice is the result. In business and politics new strategies are continually being devised that fall in the "gray zone"—the zone of confusion and disagreement about norms. This is obvious in such a simple matter as gifts. No one would argue seriously that a businessman should not send greeting cards to his customers at New Year's. But what if the greeting becomes book-length? What if it is accompanied by a bottle of Scotch? A case of champagne? Tickets for a week in Paris? (Incidentally should there be any business expenses of the kind which are tax-deductible?) The road to corruption is often paved with gifts originally unperceived as bribes. Absences of alertness and unwillingness to raise questions about aggregate consequences culminate in "scandal."

Our model of a corruption-free Utopia assumes that norms are universally applied throughout the body politic (hence that deviations do not follow lines of culture, class, interest, or personality nor vary by level of crisis). It is postulated that norms are incorporated nuclearly, not peripherally, within the personality system of each individual. If a theoretical model is to assist a detailed study of American society, it must be more complicated than our Utopian image. It must allow for the importation and local development of national differences in norms of conduct. In our society, as in all known societies, standards differ to some extent among upper-, middle-, and lower-class groups. Also interest groups frequently generate distinctive norms in every sphere of American political, economic, and social activity, and personality systems incorporate common standards to different degrees. Prescriptions are absent or diversely construed in times of prosperity and depression, war and peace, or in fact at any level of crisis.

Since the American system of public order is perpetually faced by problems that result from less than universal norms—in phraseology and deed—models that guide inquiry must explore conditions of readjustment. At the moment we shall only comment upon the *active sense of outrage*[6] that so often preconditions readjustment among norms or between articulate standards and overt action. When a collective adjustment is precipitated by a sense of outrage, few alternatives are open: either the minority norm or the inclusive norm must be changed; either the articulated norm or the pattern of deed must change. In the United States we recall many such crises; for instance the prohibition of the manufacture and sale of alcoholic beverages.

The sense of outrage is a perspective related to rectitude in which the dominant note is moral indignation. The sense of outrage may or may not be consciously perceived as justified by the violation of an explicit rule of conduct. One may in fact be seized by convictions that appear obvious; vehement affirmation, not justification, is the result. How do we relate this pattern of conduct to the maximization postulate?

The postulate does not imply that conscious processes are invariably detached, cool, and calculating; nor does it imply that the individual is explicitly aware of the value outcomes or expectations that merge in his judgment. Typically he may assume, rather than formulate, a degree of identification with other human beings, including the body politic or the legal order. The maximization postulate is a guide to the observer-analyst, leading him to probe rep-

---

[6] E. N. Kahn speaks of *The Sense of Injustice: An Anthropocentric View of Law* (New York: New York University Press, 1949) and covers a wider range of fact.

resentative cases for the purpose of uncovering the determining factors. Thus research may show that in a "housing dispute" many value outcomes are at stake; for example the reputation of the party in power, land values in particular areas, or the permeation of the community by "low-class" elements. It may be found by appropriate investigation that a particular individual is chiefly concerned about the morals of his teen-age daughter or the resale price of his home. Or a citizen may not perceive a specific, immediate stake in the situation, becoming involved in the dispute on the basis of his identification with the ideal image of a clean and decent community. In the latter case the citizen is exhibiting "disinterested moral indignation." [7]

If the observer-analyst prefers, the maximization postulate may be exclusively applied to conscious perspectives. Unconscious factors are then classified as conditions affecting the "capability" of the individual to think and act. For instance conscious indignation may be unconsciously motivated and spring from a revived childhood sense of guilt which has been remobilized in the current adult context by an allegation that police officers are seducing young girls.

Unconscious conflicts are present to some degree in all personality systems, and a sense of outrage points to deep, "whole person" involvement. In general a "sense of outrage" is aroused by disappointed expectations, such as when a norm that is expected to be lived up to is violated. Since all disappointed expectations do not evoke feelings of outrage, when does this happen?

Evidently a key factor is the *betrayal of confidence*. The original expectation about the behavior of an "other" fostered the "legitimate" assumption that the other person shared common expectations of future conduct. He promised to act in a particular way and presumably demanded of himself that he live up to shared expectations. Thus if A agrees to dispose of B's car for a 10 per cent commission and it later appears that he took 20 per cent, B presumably will feel outraged (in addition to noting and regretting the loss). In many cases there is no special understanding; for example individuals share general community expectations about the conduct of police officers. If police officers deviate, there is a sense of outrage; and the demand

---

[7] S. Ranulf worked out the dynamics of this factor in *Jealousy of the Gods and Criminal Law at Athens; A Contribution to the Sociology of Moral Indignation* (2 vols.; Copenhagen, Denmark: Einer Munksgaard Forlag, 1933-34).

for sanction may be especially intense, since betrayal by a public authority often reactivates traumatic episodes involving early experiences with family authority.

Corruption, we have said, is conditioned by "capability" as well as by "perspectives." Hence a basic hypothesis about corruption is that it is *limited by the extent to which a sense of outrage is aroused among people who are capable of making corruption more costly than correctness.* Capability depends upon the degree of control exercised over all values and is indicated by an upper, middle, or lower position in the community's distribution of power, wealth, respect, enlightenment, and other values. It is not too much to say that American society has been characterized by an endemic and occasionally acute level of largely impotent outrage.

At the level of adult relationships the sense of outrage has been generated by conflicting expectations that develop outside the centers of urban civilization. Nonurban cultures include rather extended kin groups; also rural and small-town communities. Modern urban civilization is a culture of rapidly subdividing operations that create somewhat distinctive foci of attention, demands, expectations, and identifications. Perpetual revisions of perspective set the participants off from many contemporaries, whether the contemporaries are in new circumstances or continue in earlier-type environments. As a first approximation it can be asserted that: (1) All nonurbanites are susceptible to outrage resulting from falsified expectations about urban conduct; and (2) all urbanites who develop a relatively stable subculture in a neighborhood are prone to rages that are generated by the false expectations they project upon central authorities.

We speak of impotent outrage. Declining social formations have been unable to bring about wholesale transformations of conduct on behalf of earlier norms, partly because of poor skill and insufficiently enlightened knowledge of where to concentrate; largely, perhaps, because of the vague and sweeping, almost fantasy-form, character of the image of the corrupt dragon they have sought to slay. Many of the allegedly corrupt do not perceive themselves as corrupt; they believe that they are misinterpreted by the rustic and ignorant, who they think are often misled by truly corrupt labor leaders, politicians, and politically minded clericals.

Whether we have groups or individuals in mind, the role of corruption can be grasped in its fullness only when the entire context of value and practice is considered. Any cross section in the career line of groups or individuals must be examined systematically in reference to all values and to all important patterns of practice.

The Future of Power and Rectitude: A Developmental Construct

We provide further specification of what is required in contextual analysis by examining trends and projections in the American scene as they have affected, or promise to affect, corruption or correctness. In looking to the future of American society our quest is guided to some degree by the theoretical models that have been sketched, however incompletely, for the phenomenon in question. The aim is to lay the foundation for policy recommendations concerning corruption in American life.

Full-scale developmental constructs of the future of the United States would envisage many potentialities. For present purposes we leave aside two important contingencies. One is the annihilation of America; the other is the completion of a garrison-prison polity. We pass by these constructs, partly because they have been evaluated elsewhere and partly because we wish to emphasize other implications.[8]

We focus upon the future of America and assume that the division of the world into two hostile camps continues to provide the framework in which national life is carried on.

First it will be convenient to glance directly at the institutions of government, politics, and law and assess the probable impact of future developments upon corruption and correctness. At some point in the inventory we will look directly at the institutions conventionally charged with responsibility for setting standards of rectitude and applying them to concrete cases. Our contextual approach reminds us that it is not enough to characterize power and rectitude alone; we must look at the setting. Hence we review the principal value institutions in addition to power and rectitude.

---

[8] See H. D. Lasswell, "The Garrison State," *American Journal of Sociology*, **46** (1941), 455-468; also "The Garrison State Hypothesis Today," S. P. Huntington, *Changing Patterns of Military Politics* (Glencoe, Ill.: Free Press of Glencoe, Inc., 1962); J. J. Johnson, ed., *The Role of the Military in Underdeveloped Countries* (Princeton: Princeton University Press, 1961).

Power and Power Institutions

Critics of this country have correctly said that we often approach the relatively unorganized arena of world politics with even higher ethical demands and expectations than we believe can be applied in domestic politics. Our concern for "world law," "arbitration," "renunciation of war," the League of Nations, and the United Nations is well-known. National opposition to the "destructive" use of resources has led to the notorious policy, modified only in recent times, of starving the military and naval establishments during peacetime. Opposition to "colonialism" or "imperialism" led us to feel uneasy and impure when circumstances made it necessary during recent years to cooperate with western Europe to check the expansion of Communist power. Britain, France, Belgium, Spain, and Portugal are colonial powers, and we ourselves control a number of footholds outside the territorial United States. We are bound by both an ideal of noninterference in the internal affairs of other people and a demand to conform the world picture to our ideal of self-determining nations joined within an effective frame of world public order. This conception runs into the further difficulty that we are unwilling to limit ourselves too drastically in a world arena that is characterized by a lively expectation of violence.

We rehearse these familiar points because they underline contradictions between power and rectitude that lead some groups to deny that power has any moral standing whatever; and hence whatever touches power is wholly corrupt, including measures of national security. However the crisis of national security has already introduced a new note of serious purpose, of civic responsibility, into the peacetime life of America. Military training establishes a link between the individual's career and the destiny of the body politic; and the idea of a "youth corps" formulates the desire to provide a constructive as well as a deterrent role for the rising generation. Unless specific demands upon youth succeed in winning loyalty, faith, and belief, the nation will be disunited and weakened; and the moral environment will encourage corrupt ways of evading and frustrating national progress.

Continuing stress upon the world power position of the United States will blend military and civilian professions and unify their conceptions of morality. This process is well-advanced, since the advent of modern science and technology has weakened the lines that separated the specialist on violence from the wielder of other specialized instrumentalities. The armed forces must continue their traditional preoccupation with killing and being killed; yet the complex machinery of decision-making and execution cuts down the number of men who are actively engaged in hand-to-hand combat. Professor Janowitz's checklist of civilian-type skills of the defense forces of the United States shows the transformation that has taken place.[9]

At the top of the hierarchy stand officers whose careers have been made in ways that parallel the strategies, skills, and motivations of civilian counterparts in large-scale organizations. The elite at the top of such a structure learns to focus upon the external environment of the organization. This, they find is composed of other huge structures with whose elites they engage in a perpetual dance of coalition-making and remaking. Top officials must retain a supporting coalition inside the home organization while they cultivate the connections and obtain the flow of intelligence required to operate in the larger arena where civilian and military agencies meet and where congressional committees, leaders of national pressure organizations, party bosses, and the press are in perpetual interaction with one another. Barriers between military and civilian careers are razed, since modern weapons spare no one from the target zone, and the risk is socialized.

The consequences of fusion for rectitude, although elusive, are far-reaching. The older self-image—the older loyalties, faiths, and beliefs—is no longer adequate for the multiple roles that officers are called upon to play. Careers are no longer so rigid and parochial as before, since there is contact and professional mobility across civil and military lines. The interlocking character of top elites creates many opportunities to operate in a "gray zone" where norms are uncertain. There is the tempting possibility of lucrative private employment in subcontracting firms that do business with the defense department.

Traditional taboos against "politics" are open to question in an age when defense questions are high on the agenda of public concern. What are the obligations of an officer or official who has access to

---

[9] See M. J. Janowitz, *The Professional Soldier; A Social and Political Portrait* (Glencoe, Ill.: Free Press of Glencoe, Inc., 1960).

what he considers to be vital information that is denied by his superiors to civilian executives of the Congress? Shall he maintain disciplined silence and bide his time? Shall he undermine confidence and endanger his professional career by "leaks" or even by speaking out?

The crucial conflict is rarely between the principle of civilian supremacy and the downright challenge of attempted military usurpation. The threat of a "garrison-police state" in the United States is not likely to show itself openly during ordinary mid-crisis periods. Not a "man on horseback" after the Napoleonic model, but factions composed of military-civilian-party-congressional-mass media pressuregroup elements may eventually exercise disproportionate power by cutting down public access to the information required for intelligent judgment upon security matters. Outright bribery or threat will no doubt continue to play a minor role, since men are more predisposed toward corruption by omission than toward corruption by commission.

A counteracting possibility lies in the ideological realm. It may be possible for officers to achieve a self-image that redefines their traditional concern with violent coercion against external enemies. They may prepare for a "constabulary" role, as Professor Janowitz suggests; or they may discover the potentialities in the emerging field of sanction law.[10] Specialization on instruments of armed coercion is part of the larger field of sanction; that is, of the use of value deprivations or indulgences to maintain conformity to the norms of public order. This can be called the domain of sanction law, since it relates to the management of prescriptive sanctions whether "criminal" or "civil," whether local, national, international, or global. In a broad sense specialization upon sanction is distinctive of those who study power, especially authorized and controlling power. We consider this the field of political science and recognize jurisprudence and comparative law as components. Ultimately military, police, and treatment measures will be seen as interconnecting branches of a common field of professional specialization.

It is to be anticipated that security considerations will cast their weight in favor of further centralization at the federal level. Since it

---

[10] Janowitz, *The Professional Soldier; A Social and Political Portrait*, pp. 418 ff; Arens and Lasswell, *In Defense of Public Order, The Emerging Field of Sanction Law*, especially chap. 12, "The Strategy of Sanctioning."

is difficult to meet local needs with local sources of revenue, there will probably be further centralization of state and municipal financing within the framework of federal policy.

A side effect of centralization is likely to be the elimination of the corruption-reform cycle as a prominent feature of municipal politics in this country. As was suggested before, the cycle results from decentralization and relative exemption from the play of the world balance of power.[11] When national security considerations foster unitary government with fiscal control of local financing, the preconditions of the corruption-reform cycle do not exist. In American cities, however, the cycle reflects an accommodation of conflicting and complementary interests among "rich" and "poor" wards. The poor wards include high-mobility, lodging-house districts where run-down property, which is often held for speculative purposes, usually obtains highest return when used for "immoral" purposes, especially organized prostitution and gambling. Moral standards are usually the proclaimed norms of the wealthier residential wards and of the neighborhoods abounding in children, schools, and churches. The conflicting interests in law enforcement and evasion are territorially accommodated; that is, "rackets" are resisted when they spread into "respectable" areas. The persistent pursuit of larger markets by those engaged in illegal activities, plus the chronic pressure against efficiency that results from demands for jobs and favors, tend to tip the local equilibrium against law enforcement and toward inefficiency. The resulting deprivations provoke reform crusades to restore higher levels of law enforcement, economy, and efficiency.

As the federal government becomes more deeply implicated in municipal and regional government, local cycles of corruption-reform may be transposed to the federal arena. Under the present system organized mercenary crime pays for party protection. However if legitimate business and other legitimate private interests are willing to pay for or engage in political activity, political parties can afford to sacrifice the gamblers, racketeers, and related interests. The pressure of national security interests will favor the use of national resources

---

[11] See H. D. Lasswell, *World Politics and Personal Insecurity* (New York: McGraw-Hill Book Company, Inc., 1935). Reprinted in H. D. Lasswell, C. E. Merriam, and T. V. Smith, *A Study of Power* (Glencoe, Ill.: Free Press of Glencoe, Inc., 1949).

for defense and social security and decrease inefficiency and corrupt levies.

The hand of law enforcement authorities is strengthened by new scientific instruments and procedures of detection. The reference is to wire tapping and the like. Since these devices are often abused by public officials, judges and legislators have refused to agree to full-scale employment of these means of penetrating privacy, though at the cost of considerable inefficiency in law enforcement. The conviction is deeply embedded in our legal tradition that the accused is to be protected against other than "ordinary" sources of inference concerning his motives, plans, and operations. As a matter of policy individuals are protected against surrendering certain basic "rights." For instance our legal prescriptions seek to curb overzealous officials who try to coerce confessions or who attempt to obtain evidence by raids without a warrant obtained from a judicial official; these are only two of the many safeguards of individual freedom.

Our forecast is that the motivations to use the new means of penetrating privacy will gain strength and that the protection of privacy is a losing cause. We predict, however, that the policy of giving protection to privacy will not be completely abandoned, partly because excesses will occur that shock the more sensitive leaders of the community into clarifying workable limits of penetration. The essential device is procedural and traditional: prior consultation with an independent judicial officer who must be convinced that a tentative case has been made for the invasion of privacy.

Traditional regard for privacy has already been much abridged. Many private businesses require employees to agree, as a condition of employment, to submit to lie detection tests on request; tests are called for when thefts occur. In some situations an attempt is made to put anyone who refuses to cooperate in detection procedures in an unfavorable moral position.

Up to the present time the scientific validity of polygraphs and drugs in many cases is open to serious question.[12] These limitations

---

[12] See J. Skolnick, "Scientific Theory and Scientific Evidence: An Analysis of Lie Detection," *Yale Law Journal*, **70** (1961), 694-728. On basic research developments see the papers by W. Penfield, H. Hyden, D. O. Hebb, S. S. Kety, J. G. Miller, J. O. Cole, H. A. Simon in S. M. Farber and R. H. L. Wilson, *Control of the Mind* (New York: McGraw-Hill Book Company, Inc., 1961).

will probably diminish gradually as the field of brain chemistry is better developed. Police states will not hesitate to introduce such tests into regular medical examinations, for instance, to discover ideological deviation as well as to obtain evidence of corrupt practice. Nor will they have inhibitions about employing chemical procedures to aid the indoctrination or reconstruction of individuals.[13] Although the United States will continue to experience conflicts of conscience, conflicts will probably be resolved by consent to detection, indoctrination, and treatment techniques under prescribed limitations designed to obviate abuses.

The new instruments of surveillance at the disposal of police will probably reduce corruption to the extent that corrupt acts are open to influence by measures that increase the odds against a benefit from corruption. When the norm and its sanction are clear, and the chances of detection and deprivation of an offender are high, the number of calculated violations will decrease. However, to the extent that deviations result from incapacity, including unconscious compulsivity, "certainty of punishment" will not affect the rate of deviation; in fact, if any change occurs, the rate may rise because of unconscious demands for punishment.[14]

The police forces have been profoundly affected by the technoscientific transformation of our epoch. Today they are increasingly professional and in touch with the intellectual world; and presumably there will be more progress, especially if the police, like the armed forces and many legal, political, and behavioral scientists, perceive their common role in terms of sanction law.

In our view the principal impact of technology upon corruption will not be made by the numerous specialized gadgets for detecting offenses. We are already in the early stages of the computer revolution.[15] The explosive development of computational machines now

---

[13] Consult A. M. Meerloo, *The Rape of the Mind* (Cleveland: World Publishing Co., 1956); W. W. Sargant, *Battle for the Mind* (New York: Doubleday & Company, Inc., 1957).

[14] The classical treatment of this theme is F. Alexander and H. Staub, *The Criminal and His Judge* (New York: The Macmillan Company, 1931).

[15] For technical details about computers consult H. D. Huskey and G. A. Korn, eds., *Computer Handbook* (New York: McGraw-Hill Book Company, Inc., 1960). New developments in related fields can be followed in *M.U.L.L.*, quarterly newsletter of the American Bar Association Special Committee on Electronic Data Retrieval in collaboration with Yale Law School.

makes it feasible to simulate social and physical processes in detail and at great speed. It is, for example, already possible to use machines to simulate the flow of economic transactions, including payments for tax purposes, and to call attention to any disproportionality. It is practicable to simulate the flow of offers and acceptances in a market and to spot events that may result from corrupt practice. For instance lack of flexibility among bidders points to the possibility of collusion. This presumption is heightened if input-output simulation establishes the fact that striking differences in cost of production exist among bidders. The entire accounting system of selected concerns can be examined in relation to comparable businesses.

It was an important step toward commercial and fiscal integrity when double-entry bookkeeping was invented and when written records, including receipted bills and other corroborative detail, were required. It was, in fact, an important step toward honesty in government, business, and other social institutions when verbatim transcripts became part of the public records of legislatures, administrative hearings, court proceedings, and the like. In the future the records will be far more detailed and they will be promptly processed in simulations that cover every value-shaping and value-sharing process in society. Expectations will be precisely organized concerning the "proportions" to be anticipated at every phase of interaction among groups of individuals.

In many ways the most profound result of the simulation of American social process will be the exposure of ambiguities in the statement of accepted norms. Legislators and administrators will be faced with precisely formulated questions about *which* policy operationally specifies the norm. Furthermore they will be aided in coming to a conclusion by simulations of the aggregate consequences for all values and institutions of choosing one specification system or another. Suppose, for example, that no "favored treatment" is to be given by business A to any business that is wholly or partly owned by A or which has more than a 5 per cent participation by any individual or organization with a 5 per cent participation in A. What would be the cost of obtaining a stated degree of compliance with this proposed norm? Cost could be computed in terms of several values: for instance money expended on specialized enforcement activities; increased noncompliance in enforcement activities neglected as a result of concentrating resources on the present task; consequences of any increased noncompliance in terms of accidents and other deprivations of safety, health, and comfort; consequences of the proposed policy for reducing the degree of monopolistic control exercised by top family groups, financial corporations, and industrial corporations; increased political hostility against the party in power as expressed in business and other journals and among prospective campaign contributors; fewer corrupt practices among the buyers and sellers of raw materials, semiprocessed and processed goods, and services; increased scientific and public attention to the problem of monopolistic control of American economic life; increased expressions of respect for buyers and sellers as a group with genuine professional standards, and heightened identification with such careers.

Although the foregoing items do not provide an exhaustive inventory of the reverberations likely to follow from any policy alternative, they do call attention to an important implication of the contextual approach to any policy question; namely, the deliberate use of a comprehensive social-process map as a means of bringing to mind pertinent features of the whole. "Increased noncompliance" and "decreased corrupt practices" refer to rectitude; "deprivations of safety, health, and comfort" to well-being; "degree of monopolistic control" to power and wealth; "political hostility" to power; "increased scientific and public attention" to skill and enlightenment; "increased respect" and "heightened identification" to respect and affection. These attributions are first approximations only, since detailed follow-through would bring out the degree to which each interaction involves every value.[16]

Simulations of power and rectitude interactions can make pertinent, though provisional, presentations of policy alternatives available and can expedite the discovery and removal of ambiguous norms and the assessments of the net value consequences of policy.

A centralized government will be the largest organized component of American society; it is likely to be larger, more permeating, and far more all-seeing than the federal establishment of today. The spectacle of big organization already haunts the mind of modern man. A major concern is corruption and correctness; and the principal

---

[16] H. D. Lasswell, "The Interplay of Economic, Political and Social Criteria in Legal Policy," *Vanderbilt Law Review*, **14** (1961), 451-471.

threat of huge administrative structures is that "sins of omission," rather than "sins of commission," will characterize the impersonal, subdivided, automatized operations of officialdom. A dim line separates caution and sloth from more obvious deviations from responsible conduct.

The folk image of the bureaucrat has long since depicted every nuance of this familiar role. There is the timid official who is willing to let refugees stay in the rain because he has no authority to admit uncertified people into an empty building; the devotee of red tape who denies hospital facilities to an expectant mother because she left a vaccination certificate at home; the man who cowers at the mention of an influential figure and gives preference where none is justified; the pint-sized tyrant who does not like somebody's face and lets him sit to the end of the day when it is too late to act; and many more portrayals of the infirmities of human character.

The fate of many institutions is determined in the thousands and millions of day-to-day confrontations that impose deprivations or grant indulgences—petty or great—upon all who are involved. The process is two-way. Organization men themselves are involved as well as the client or the customer, who in other roles are also organization men. Human personality as shaped by the playing of official roles is but partly understood, although we have innumerable indications that point to some provisional conclusions.

Methods are available today for describing the impact of organization upon personality and of personality upon organization. Methods are available for discovering the impact of an organization upon extra-organizational contacts, whether the levels are elite-to-elite, mid-elite, or rank-and-file-to-rank-and-file. By proper interviewing and participant observation we can learn for the first time the nature of the face that government presents to the community, and by proper sampling we can acquire data capable of providing relevant magnitudes for the simulators.[17]

---

[17] On the study of organization see M. Weber, *The Theory of Social and Economic Organization* (New York: Oxford University Press, 1947). A contemporary approach is J. G. Marsh and H. A. Simon, *Organizations* (New York: John Wiley & Sons, Inc., 1958). On many problems of big-scale organizations and norms see C. Argyris, *Personality and Organization* (New York: Harper & Row, Publishers, 1957); A. Etzioni, *A Comparative Analysis of Complex Organizations* (Glencoe, Ill.: Free Press of Glencoe, Inc., 1961).

The use of simulation to provide built-in flexibility is part of the problem of preventing corrupt practice. Simulation procedures need not freeze social practice in uncrackable molds. We indicated how machine processing, by exposing suspicious rigidities, such as in bidding, paves the way for greater flexibility. Similarly simulations can reveal tendencies toward rigidity in big-scale administration and call attention to the probable need of flexibility. Modern pioneers in personnel selection tend to choose an individual according to his degree of conformance to the patterns of those people who have succeeded in the past. This has been true of admissions to officer-training schools and schools of public administration and of promotions within all services. If such a policy continues, it becomes "self-fulfilling," since anyone who falls outside the preferred profile is rejected. We can, however, build a requirement of "ten per cent risk" into our selection procedures—a requirement which instructs personnel officers to take a chance on promising prospects who fall outside the built-in profiles.

Simulation methods can be used to expose and counteract the effect of stereotyped experience during career development. Officials are needed who move back and forth between "public," "nonprofit private," and "private profit" activities. Men and women who stay with one official "ladder" and occupy several places are also needed.

The size of government in tomorrow's civilization makes it imperative to reconsider more than one established canon of administrative practice. For years we have stressed the "neutrality" of civil servant and officer, partly as a strategy for the protection of public order against corruption. It is not rational to quarrel with the proposition that career men in government must be willing to serve the "policy" heads of the establishment and to recognize the legal and ethical responsibility of these heads to the body politic. The top man must be able to rely upon the professional competence and integrity of the great administrative mechanisms at his disposal.

Every experienced person knows that there are "gray zones" in the application of the norm of deference to the political head. The top man may be judged a fool by the career man; and the career man may with all sincerity of devotion to the public interest do what he can to nullify the damage that the fool can do to the national interest before recurring electoral storms clear the air again. In theory, we are told, the career man ought to take leave or resign and leave the fool to early exposure and elimination; but this is a price that is unbearably high for many career men who lack private income and have not cultivated a university or business cushion on which to make an emergency landing.

There will probably be more forthright recognition of the limited application of the "neutrality" norm in the future. As big government expands, its role in society will expand: the number of employees of government will multiply; the number of businesses that depend upon government contracts, of universities and educational institutions that rely upon government aid to scholarship and research, of hospitals and charitable activities that use official facilities, and of mass media that depend upon government sources of information and advertising income from businesses vulnerable to government will multiply. Shall we prohibit citizens who are employed by government or heavily involved with government from advocating public policy, from correcting factual misstatements made to the public, from contributing to pressure groups and political parties, from running for office? Public discussion will die out in this country if the policy of "neutrality" is carried to extremes. Instead of contributing to efficiency and honest government it is more likely to prepare the ground for inefficiency, corruption, and autocracy.

Several working solutions of these difficulties are in sight and can be expected to spread. First is the role of the professional association. More and more public employees belong to organizations of government employees and to associations of fellow professionals in scientific and scholarly fields. These organizations can engage in research and issue policy statements for the guidance of general opinion. If security limitations prevent the publication of the factual grounds of inference, the community is at least enabled to obtain expressions of judgment which have been disciplined by exposure to relevant facts and estimates. Public employees can and should participate actively in public life in ways that will compensate for the taboos of their official roles. An organization's report need not be signed by individuals; it is sufficient to have a reputable professional channel serve as sponsor.[18] Liberal leaves of absence must be available to officials who desire to run for office or to take part in active party politics.

---

[18] In Great Britain the Fabian Society developed a good reputation for the competence and reliability of what it had to say about government. Civil servants helped to prepare its publications.

The preceding discussion of the problems raised by big administration has led us away from emphasizing a development in government that is likely to be affected by the use of computers in the simulation of past, present, and future events. We refer to the sharper
definition and separation of various functions in the decision process.

There has been a growth in independence of organs relatively specialized to intelligence (including planning) and to appraisal functions. By the intelligence function we mean the gathering and processing of information needed by decision-makers for planning the future.
The appraisal function could be merged with intelligence; but the
study of comparative government indicates that the appraisal task is
so important politically that it requires distinctive identity and special
safeguarding precautions. Appraisers report on the degree to which
past policy goals and methods have accomplished their stated purpose. The judgment need not be "global"; that is, it need not sum up
by saying that our military or social security programs were failures or
successes. However appraisers can provide the basis for such inferences
by raising questions and reporting results separately on each item.

The man or the organ in charge of facts and estimates is in a
potent position. A combination of fortunate circumstances made it
possible for the judiciary to establish its independence in England and
to transmit the institution to the United States and other nations.[19]
A similarly fortunate concatenation of factors is required before the
independence of the appraiser can be fully established. Top executives and legislators have long resisted the independence of the appraiser and have shut his mouth or cut off his working facilities with
relative impunity. High standards of competence of social and behavioral scientists will be more obvious to fellow scientists and to
laymen when they master the machine as an instrument adapted to
simulate past and prospective contingencies. As their credibility rises,
they will be in a stronger position to insist that the results of their
work be made available to all participants in the decision process.
Controversies will continue to arise, since those who recognize
their vulnerability will invent new ways of limiting freedom of appraisal. But in a society whose members are more cognizant of the
methods of scientific inquiry and the significance of machine simula-

---

[19] For further information about the independent judiciary see E. McWhin-
ney, *Judicial Review in the English-speaking World* (Toronto: U. of Toronto
Press, 1956).

tion, the chances are high that the independent role of intelligence and appraisal will be accepted.

This development is especially important to the party and pressure-group systems and the role of mass electorates. As scientific knowledge expands, the manipulation of news and comment for special purposes will be based upon more and more exhaustive information about the predispositions of the electorate. Voting studies conducted by political scientists have already made available a vast stock of knowledge about the American electorate; and machine simulation has begun.[20] If this knowledge is not to be exploited for special, including corrupt, purposes, it must be made available to all.

We propose that the general principle that applies here is that *manipulators and manipulated should have common access to knowledge about predispositions.* Survey and simulation results should be, and probably will be, publicly accessible. Access may be achieved by many supplementary devices. To some extent government agencies can be used to provide past and contemporary data and interpretation. Private nonprofit organs may be set up or used for the purpose. It may be regarded as acceptable for new results to be reported after brief delay to encourage the application of talent to the disclosure of ever more subtle factors that condition judgment.

These procedures apply not only to the electorate, but also to every official or organ in the decision process of any body politic. The higher courts and other important tribunals have long been targets of systematic as well as haphazard forecasting; and today machine simulation will soon provide more exhaustive grounds of prediction. There are advantages in making such knowledge available to legislators, administrators, officials, and voters. Such exposure will increase the possibility of self-understanding and insight by making everyone aware of unnoted and unevaluated biases. If these biases are brought into the open, the prospects of improved insight are increased. Insight, not prediction, is the principal contribution of social and behavioral science to judgment.

A well-known source of corruption in government is the person or organ which has the combined function of advocacy and judgment.

---

[20] See I. de Sola Pool and R. Abelson, "The Simulmatics Project," *Public Opinion Quarterly,* XXV (1961), 167-183; W. N. McPhee, "Note on a Campaign Simulator," *Public Opinion Quarterly,* XXV (1961), 184-193.

Although some men are able to judge wisely in their own cases, bias usually creeps in. Our institutions have separated advocacy from judgment in judicial affairs by providing for a judiciary independent of the executives who initiate prosecutions or appear in civil suits. Regulatory commissions are well-advised to organize their work in such a way that "rule-making" is distinguished from "initiation of complaints" and "hearing and judgment of complaints." [21] Our legislative bodies, and especially the Congress, rarely feel that they are bound to make such a separation. If the right of a member to sit is challenged, it is generally considered inappropriate for him to be on the committee that decides the matter; there are perhaps shadowy limitations upon the propriety of a committee member voting on matters mainly concerned with his own lands or corporations; and there are vague restrictions upon practicing a profession during one's incumbency. But it is acceptable for a legislator to use his position to vote for policies supported by his constituents from which they obviously hope to obtain a relatively greater benefit than other parts of the country. Will this be regarded as corrupt practice when moral sensibility is more refined? Legislators who are committed to territorial interests will be free to advocate their commitment, but they will be disqualified from voting or trading. In this way certain recommending and invoking functions will be distinguished from one another and from prescribing and applying functions.

Many well-known deviations from democratic principles will probably be corrected in the years immediately ahead. For example formal and effective suffrage discriminations against Negroes are becoming obsolete. The white caste will modify its outlook in coming years and accept the rise of the Negro component of American society.

The moral tone of American politics will undoubtedly be affected by the dissolution of ancient injustice. Citizens of sensitive conscience will take renewed pride in the national record as "hypocrisy" becomes a thing of the past. Nevertheless the transition will

---

[21] For recent examinations of regulatory institutions see M. H. Bernstein, *Regulating Business by Independent Commission* (Princeton: Princeton University Press, 1955); and especially M. S. Massel, *Competition and Monopoly; Legal and Economic Issues* (Washington, D. C.: The Brookings Institution, 1962); also E. S. Mason, ed., *The Corporation in Modern Society* (Cambridge, Mass.: Harvard University Press, 1960); J. M. Clark, *Competition As a Dynamic Process* (Washington, D. C.: The Brookings Institution, 1961).

continue to be rough in those communities where grudging changes occur as a result of "outside pressure." It is always possible to organize strong rearguard action against "interference" as a means of defending the traditional freedom to choose a scapegoat. "Foreigners"— whether from Europe or New York—provide an acceptable enemy against whose machinations all strategies, even corruption, can be defended.

As we have said in the discussion of theoretical models, old norms may not seem to apply in novel situations, and inner conflicts may exert disproportionate control over the first solutions that occur. When previously low-status groups are put into higher positions, their accumulated resentment may be expressed in corrupt conduct. To the newly emancipated the sense of injustice sometimes seems to provide ample justification for seizing neglected opportunities for enrichment. The new leadership may be able to count upon the norm-lessness of the new constituents.

So far as American Negro minorities are concerned, countervailing factors are present in the situation. The Negro has been emancipated piecemeal, and in the cities of the North elite and mid-elite elements have been developed which are slowly merging with the community at large. In the South the process has been held back, and Negro leadership in the southern states will probably demonstrate many of the corrupt traits referred to above.

Another change directly affecting democratic institutions will be the modification of built-in discriminations against populous areas. Such discriminations have spawned a host of petty privileges which invite corruption. Many business enterprises[22] which operate in multistate markets and are vulnerable to regulation treat the funds required for corruption as a regular cost of business. Many politicians in over-represented districts yield to the temptation offered by nationwide special interests to sell their votes. When poverty and lack of education are combined with the franchise, the vote is one of the few negotiable assets available to the hard-pressed citizen of the nation's neglected regions. The tragic irony is that the bargaining position of the overrepresented district does not necessarily attract public or private funds for investments that raise the social capital of the com-

---

[22] Data concerning areas and population are in Lane, *Political Life*; *Why People Get Involved in Politics*, sec. 1.

munity. Instead the petty elite that specializes in political manipulation may oppose expenditures that would transform the social structure of the community and thereby create new elements who would drive the corruptionists out of power. Entrenched local elements often consider preservation of the old order vital to their interests. They may fear the rise of the trade union influence if industry is allowed to expand as well as alien managers and owners who would undermine the "peculiar institutions" sheltered by the local culture. If the local culture is based upon the requirements of a white caste, as in many communities of the South, modernization may be checked for years.

One of the most notorious cases of overrepresentation is the "dying wards" of cities. In this situation also the acquiescence of the nation to antidemocratic practice fosters corruption. Furthermore it is precisely in these wards that the failure of the local community as a whole has been most apparent. Vanishing wards have long been the sites of the most dilapidated housing and the least adequate public services. The political elite of specialists on political manipulation have sold their influence, not for vast programs of investment and modernization, but for disposable income which is invested elsewhere or is directed into local counter-mores enterprises (e.g., gambling, prostitution, narcotics).

The influence buyers in these districts are often the elements who are most reluctant to transform the community. They may, for example, fear industry and therefore support stores, office buildings, hotels, and apartments which present less competition for control than new factories.

There is nothing fixed about such interpretations of interest; and in emerging America the vanishing wards will also probably vanish as metropolitan and regional plans catch up with the social changes that for many years left national initiative far behind the maps of potentiality.[23]

The forecast is that many antidemocratic practices built into the effective constitutions of federal, state, and local governments will dis-

---

[23] For the reawakened concern with cities see W. Kornhauser, *The Politics of Mass Society* (Glencoe, Ill.: Free Press of Glencoe, Inc., 1959); J. S. Coleman, *Community Conflict* (Glencoe, Ill.: Free Press of Glencoe, Inc., 1957); W. Sayre and H. Kaufman, *Governing New York City: Politics in the Metropolis* (New York: Russell Sage Foundation, 1960).

solve and that many situations conducive to corruption will be no more. Also the shortened working day, combined with rising levels of culture, and a continuing mood of civic responsibility in the face of danger will attract more Americans of high character and skill into the political arena.

Chapter Four

The Emerging Social Context

Wealth and Wealth Institutions

The relatively sanguine view of the future that we have been sketching does not blind us to the strong disposition to corrupt practice under various circumstances, especially when there appears to be an excellent prospect of getting away with it. Looking now at the business world, we are immediately reminded of the never-ending struggle between monopoly and competition, including the disposition to circumvent legal limitations on private monopoly. Adam Smith was aware of the truisms that competition, when left to itself, becomes monopoly through conspiracy and that monopolists conspire to maintain monopoly. The propensity to conspire rises from well-known factor combinations that recur throughout a system of markets. Competition implies the risk of the future recoverability of investment. The investor may be taken by surprise when a new product appears or when a price cut is made possible by new modes of production. The consuming public may redefine demand and suffer a seizure of fashion that nullifies past calculations and commitments. Many enterprisers are more concerned with cutting down capital risk than with making a quick profit. Competitors are frequently more aware of the possibility of limiting the losses they are able to impose upon one another than of the safeguarding of gains. All these expectations

93

and demands strengthen the "long-term" tendency to transform competition into monopoly.

The public policy of America has long been committed to the wisdom of competitive business—a policy that deliberately contradicts the cumulative strength of the many dispositions toward monopoly. The ideological considerations in America's antimonopoly program can be summarized in the statement that a democratic polity cannot survive private monopoly: either the monopolist becomes the government, or the government becomes the monopolist; if the monopolist becomes the government, autocracy prevails; if the government becomes the monopolist, bureaucracy becomes a caste.

In response to the antitrust programs of the American commonwealth some businessmen have developed a special ideology that can be dignified as a philosophy of corruption. Justifications of corruption are well-recognized, but *sotto voce*. The argument is: The incorruptibility of public and private persons is an ideal toward which we aspire; it cannot, however, be achieved in many practical situations without exposing businesses to great and unwarranted risk. Corruption can legitimately be used to mitigate excessive competition—cutthroat competition—without going to the extreme of full monopoly, which in turn provokes government monopoly and sooner or later leads to autocracy. Corruption is a means of maintaining the many advantages of the modern organization of markets into patterns composed of a few leading firms and many small units.[1]

The rapid expansion of private business during the latter years of the nineteenth century was accompanied by bribery and other forms of corruption. The Civil War left many men with broken and disturbed careers, and they were eager to enrich themselves after having sacrificed to the collective good. The period exhibited the corruption of an expanding economy inspired by the fabulous resources and windfalls of a sparsely inhabited continent. The connection between brigandage and economics was never closer than when waves of

---

[1] Fragmentary clues to the ideology of businessmen are provided in R. E. Lane, *Regulation of Business Men* (New Haven: Yale University Press, 1954). On proposed norms of official-unofficial conduct see *Conflict of Interest and Federal Service; The Association of the Bar of the City of New York Special Committee on the Federal Conflict of Interest Laws* (Cambridge, Mass.: Harvard University Press, 1960).

snatchers and grabbers rolled across the Mississippi and eventually reached the Pacific coast. After explorers, trappers, scouts, and herders came railroaders and miners; eventually there was settlement and order. The nation was left with a confused and contradictory ideology; it praised saints, pirates, men of peace, and strong, capable captains of industry and finance. By the beginning of the twentieth century the territorial map was established and the nation began to discover frontiers in science, technology, and business consolidation and subtler strategies of management and legal manipulation.

The most potent instrument of attack upon business corruption in future years has been suggested above; namely, the simulation of economic and social processes under the direction of theorists who specialize in the study of aggregate social process and who guide the computers that exhibit the flow in detail.

No one can overlook the disappearance of incentives to corruption that were formerly nourished by poverty and joblessness. Our economy has already made vast changes in the income position of the lower third of the population and effectively, if not formally, guarantees at least minimum economic security. We are committed to an affluent, dynamic, unemployment-free economy; and whatever stands in the way will be swept aside.[2]

Corruption, however, is not the monopoly of poverty-stricken voters and petty officials who sell themselves to lobbyists and bosses. Modern economic society specializes upon the arts of arousing demand. Possessing scientific and technical potential for the production of goods and services on a fabulous scale, it increases demand through advertising, merchandising, and planning attractive items for the market. These devices invoke value appeals of every kind and trans-

---

[2] A brief reminder of the striking trends exhibited by the American economy: In 1929 over half the households in this country were receiving less than $3,000 annually, and a little more than 15 per cent received between $5,000 and $9,999; in 1960 nearly 20 per cent of the households received under $3,000 and over 40 per cent had incomes ranging from $5,000 to $10,000. See National Planning Association, Planning Pamphlet No. 107 (1959). For a different interpretation of trends consult M. Harrington, *The Other America: Poverty in the United States* (New York: The Macmillan Company, 1962); G. Kolko, *Wealth and Power in America* (New York: Frederick A. Praeger, Inc., 1962); J. N. Morgan and others, *Income and Welfare in the United States* (New York: McGraw-Hill Book Company, Inc., 1962).

form the simplest purchase into a matter of respect, affection, economic advancement, health, knowledge, know-how, morality, and patriotism. A "side effect" is the promotion of corruption, since consumer indebtedness is encouraged and criteria of self-respect demand the sacrifice of morals for income.[3]

Coupled with these developments is more leisure from work, at least for the principal income source.[4] There is more time for enjoyment, spending, and consumption, and such time encourages "fun" rather than "thrift" and incorruptibility. A principal consequence of the "materialistic" stress on money is gambling. The United States is apparently moving from an economy of work and speculation toward an economy of minimum work, maximum leisure, speculation, and gambling.

This trend poses difficult policy questions, since American society contains many traditional elements who look upon gambling as corrupt and are determined to keep the government from corrupting its own citizens. However, strong social forces are working in the opposite direction. Many cultural traditions that have been imported into America take government control of gambling for granted. Also the pressure to raise charitable and public funds multiplies the incentives to legalize gambling.[5]

One of the changes affecting the future of business, power, and rectitude is the spreading sense of responsibility among owners and managers. This self-consciousness is reflected in many ways; notably, in the frequent discussion of the social responsibilities of business in books, articles, conferences, and reports to stockholders. Corporations have taken such tangible steps as making grants for research and

[3] Embezzlement is an offense that appeals to ambitious "white-collar" people. See D. R. Cressey, *Other People's Money* (Glencoe, Ill.: Free Press of Glencoe, Inc., 1953); E. H. Sutherland, *White Collar Crime* (New York: Holt, Rinehart & Winston, Inc., 1949).

[4] One measure of leisure is length of vacation; and vacations have lengthened since 1945 by 150 per cent while the population has increased by 25 per cent. See footnote 2. For path-breaking approach to a traditional cliché see S. De Grazia, *Of Time, Work, and Leisure* (New York: The Twentieth Century Fund, 1962).

[5] On gambling see J. Cohen and M. Hansel, *Risk and Gambling: The Study of Subjective Probability* (New York: Philosophical Library, 1956); H. Chafetz, *Play the Devil; A History of Gambling in the U. S. from 1492 to 1955* (New York: Clarkson N. Potter, Inc., 1960); M. Ploscowe and E. J. Lukas, eds., "Gambling," *Annals of the American Academy of Political and Social Science* (Philadelphia, 1950), Vol. 269.

education and creating personal foundations for public purposes.[6]
Business leaders who talk the vernacular of social responsibility
are often accused of deliberately misrepresenting their purpose. In the
United States the traditional view of the courts has been that business
is supposed to make money for the stockholders; therefore no outlay
is legitimate unless a probable link can be shown between the expenditure and the asset position of the stockholders. The freedom of
the managers to pursue policies that will undoubtedly strengthen their
own position, whether the policies benefit stockholders or not, depends upon the extent to which the courts accept comprehensive interpretations of stockholders' interests. Thus instead of making dis-
bursements to the government as "taxes," expenditures are called
legitimate "costs" or "reinvestment." One result is a "public relations" payoff in the sense that opinion leaders and government officials look favorably upon the business and its leaders as enlightened
benefactors of the educational, scientific, cultural, and private welfare of the community. A reputation of this kind is considered important; for example it presumably can help to stave off regulative or
expropriation measures against an industry, to forestall adverse comment, and to reduce possible boycott in case of labor-management
controversies.

It is possible to object to "liberal" interpretations of stockholders' interest by arguing that market criteria are the appropriate standards for public policy to support and that only the decision-makers
of the community have the authority to specify other goals of the
commonwealth and to incur the responsibility of allocating community resources to these goals.[7] Allowing private business managers
to withhold taxes and choose the recipients of these funds as grants
is tantamount to the government's abdicating its proper responsibility

---

[6] The support of research in the United States is a practice of great and
growing importance: In 1930 when the gross national product was less than one
hundred billion dollars, the disbursement for research and development totaled
two hundred million dollars. By 1960 the gross national product was about five
times the earlier figure, and expenditure for research and development was above
ten billion. The National Science Foundation reports currently on the financing
of research.

[7] Dean E. V. Rostow of the Yale Law School has recently supported the
traditional view in *Planning for Freedom: The Public Law of American Capitalism* (New Haven: Yale University Press, 1959).

to the community as a whole. In effect public authority is being improperly delegated to private persons.

A similar argument is used against the alleged abuse of the mechanism of the nonprofit foundation. Voting control can be perpetuated in a family foundation and used to divert funds to the foundation; these funds ought to be disbursed to stockholders or routed to eventual recipients by community grants rather than by private allocators. The conclusion is that the claim of social responsibility and the overuse of the foundation device are employed as subterfuges, or conspirative arrangements, designed to weaken the power of public authorities for the benefit of industrial and financial oligarchy. This is a novel twist in the never-ceasing struggle of special interests to undermine those who are directly authorized to interpret the interests of the whole community.

Up to the present there has been little effective criticism of the recipients of business funds. However general acquiescence need not continue indefinitely. State educational institutions, for example, may enter into coalition with the representatives of other "tax-supported" institutions and claim that "private" institutions are, in fact, "tax-supported," even though they are invisibly supported by "tax exemptions" that enable the private donor rather than the public legislator and administrator to select the channel and aim. It may be argued that the social responsibility of business is to cede the control of funds for public purposes to the direct representatives of the whole community. The argument may be supported by allegations of corruption that takes the subtle form of vested interests among scholars and scientists who overlook, or play down, the public interest conflicts involved.

It is pertinent to examine the moralistic attacks against businessmen and the business system in historical perspective. This perspective, incidentally, is likely to become more common than it has been in the past, not only because business spokesmen will see that they have something to gain by it, but also because the level of knowledge about history and society is likely to be much improved—points to which we return at a later stage. For the present we recall that ever since commerce, industry, and finance emerged in urban societies, there has been unceasing complaint about the dulled moral sensibility of all who engage in "nonproductive" activities. In the perspective of cultural evolution, folk societies preceded civilizations, and civilizations arose when cities were invented.[8] The city is a complex division of labor that emphasizes values other than unswerving loyalty to the kinship group. The state rather than the family or tribe became the dominant social unit, and individuals and pluralistic groups were freed to pursue wealth, skill, enlightenment, power, and other values so long as the requirements of the state were not contravened. Private trading and manufacture and private financing were encouraged, within limits, by urban-centered states, since the resulting tax revenues usually yielded a higher net than those of enterprises administered directly by paid officials. Businessmen learned to think impersonally in terms of dollars, prices, and margins and to plan; they disciplined impulse by calculation and often rejected an unprofitable claim which was put forward in the name of the age-old norms of a folk society. Many contemporary antibusiness ideologies have their historical genesis in the cultural shock of civilization *versus* folk. Even in societies dominated by urban perspectives and ways a minority of relatively less urbanized elements sneers at the "nonproductive" life of cities.

The fate of private business as a social institution depends in part upon the strategies of businessmen and business organizations. American businessmen will probably seek to survive, not by a strategy of masterful dictation, but by subtler strategies that depend upon winning public acceptance of their image of responsibility. The elite of private business are aware that the alternative to a business system is a bureaucratic state; in the latter the military, police, and administrative elites are dominant, and such elites in turn may give rise to the ascendancy of factions recruited from scientific and technical elites. In the contemporary world private business is too weak to indulge in strategies of contempt for responsible conduct.

The Enlightenment Value
and Enlightenment Institutions

Our examination of rectitude and power has repeatedly emphasized the important role of enlightenment in determining the ef-

---

[8] See V. G. Childe, *What Happened in History* (New York: Penguin Books, Inc., 1946); Robert Redfield, *The Primitive World and Its Transformations* (Ithaca: Cornell University Press, 1953).

fective context of social interaction. We emphasized the "confusion" that so often accompanies change, noting that the confusion involves not only ambiguity of norms, but also vagueness in "matters of fact." When we speak of enlightenment as a value, we refer to maps of expectation pertaining to past, present, and prospective events in the world of nature and man.

It is commonplace to comment upon the impact of science and technology upon man's view of himself in the universe. In this connection we do not refer to the disruption of older ways of life, but to the extensive transformation of ancient perspectives. The rate of accumulation of knowledge from observation puts a great burden upon man's outlook.

Current confusions are exemplified in the stresses felt by intellectuals. C. P. Snow graphically presented the situation in terms of "The Two Cultures"; and traditional "humanists" are often out of harmony with the advance of science, especially since the social and behavioral sciences are invading the domain of humanism.

Of what importance is the divided mind of the intellectual world to the state of virtue or corruption in American society? The intellectual community has failed to anticipate the upcoming problems in our society and thereby allowed an unnecessary sense of chaos to shape the minds and outlook of many members of both younger and older generations. As yet the policy sciences challenge—the challenge to a truly configurative approach—has been but partially taken up. The task of establishing an intelligence and appraisal process that will guide the community has been tackled with less zeal than the present critical posture of life amply justifies. Too many members of the intellectual community, finding that they are unable to penetrate the new world of science, admit their private limitations in litanies of whining futility.

At the same time integrative tendencies gain strength and germinate institutions better adapted to the contemporary environment. We refer, for instance, to the adaptation of the "center" mechanism to the world of higher learning. A "center" is a small congregation of scholars who know one another and communicate on intellectual matters. In fact the idea of a "center" is an attempt to revivify the idea of a university—an ideal that has been attenuated in modern times by the proliferation of special fields of inquiry. The great universities of the United States have tended to become common mailing addresses for congeries of separate enterprises which have little intellectual contact with one another. Many innovators have asked whether it is possible to supplement this development by providing a situation where, besides pursuing particular studies, scholars share a common concern for the place of intellectual institutions in society. The "center" device favors the growth of a self-image among intellectuals based upon a comprehensive view of history, the social process, and the probable course of future events—in a word the configurative approach that we advocate and to some extent exemplify in this book.

The skills of modern science and technology are beginning to provide scholars with equipment supple enough to assist in the huge integrative undertaking required to cope with the problems of mankind. Teaching machines, for example, are a new leap forward in the cultivation of talent.[9] We have already celebrated in these pages the vast significance of the computer revolution.

It would be a gross perversion of reality if we were to imply that academic institutions or the existing academic community are uncontaminated by practices that border upon corruption. The relatively modest economic position of college and university personnel suggests that if corruption does exists, it is more subtle than the peculation of funds. Is it corrupt to pretend to be someone other than one knows one's self to be in fact? If so, an astonishing number of men and women who purport to be intellectuals are impostors. In candid discussions with friends and in clinical interviews they admit that whatever spark they once had has been extinguished and that they are simply "making a living." Satisfactory estimates of the extent of this internal disaffection from the nominal role of intellectuals in civilization are not available. One index of the general situation is the fact that the doctoral dissertation is the sole attempt of most doctors of philosophy to contribute directly to the advancement of knowledge and to the enrichment of the legacy of one generation to

[9] See E. B. Fry, G. L. Bryan, and J. W. Rigney, "Teaching Machines: An Annotated Bibliography," *Audio-Visual Communication Review*, **8** (1960), No. 2; A. A. Lumsdaine and R. Glaser, eds., *Teaching Machines and Programmed Learning* (Washington, D. C.: National Education Association, 1960).

the next. Some candid self-appraisals are in progress, and this is a hopeful sign.[10]

Why have American scholars failed to investigate many obvious and important phenomena in our civilization? Social research has been accused of investigating whomever the researcher can look down upon. Since the typical provenience of social and behavioral scientists is middle-class, the preferred targets of inquiry have been bums, prostitutes, petty criminals, and fellow occupants of the lower strata of society. The plutocrats, members of the social elite, statesmen, top scientists and intellectuals, and religious and moral leaders are relatively overlooked; or, it is alleged, they have been approached with a lack of sympathy that reflects an ambivalent class perspective toward elites—a perspective characteristic of class hostility or renegadism.

Since there has been a recent redirection of research toward elites, the complaint referred to has lost validity. At the same time any competent study of the role of intellectuals in American society must draw attention to ideological factors that affect and often distort results. For instance the famous study of *The Authoritarian Personality* betrayed an unmistakable bias in favor of the "Left." [11]

The traditional obligation of a professional man is to go beyond the possession of skill to the cultivation of enlightenment. He is expected to identify the common interest and to speak up for it rather than sell all his talent to the highest bidder for purposes dictated by that bidder. The physician, for instance, is expected to take an interest in the health of the community and to demonstrate this interest by giving advice on matters of public health as well as by serving a fringe of charity cases. The lawyer is expected to act as an agent of the community and the court and to limit his representation of the client's special interest to the permissible advocacy provided by the recognized standards of the established system. Clergymen and educators are assumed to be available for civic activities and

---

[10] See B. Berelson, *Graduate Education in the U. S.* (New York: McGraw-Hill Book Company, Inc., 1960); T. Caplow and R. J. McGee, *The Academic Marketplace* (New York: Basic Books, Inc., 1958); P. F. Lazarsfeld, W. Thielens, and D. Riesman, *The Academic Mind; Social Scientists in a Time of Crisis* (Glencoe, Ill.: Free Press of Glencoe, Inc., 1958).

[11] See E. A. Shils, "Authoritarianism: 'Right' and 'Left,'" R. Christie and M. Jahoda, eds., *Studies in the Scope and Method of "The Authoritarian Personality"* (Glencoe, Ill.: Free Press of Glencoe, Inc., 1954); also E. A. Shils, *Torment of Secrecy* (Glencoe, Ill.: Free Press of Glencoe, Inc., 1956).

to relinquish many opportunities for personal enrichment. However many physicians, lawyers, and engineers give exclusive service to the special interests of rich, private clients. The professional ideal has been corrupted by the triumph of the profit-seeking imperative.[12] The value conflict among many professional men is symptomatic of the stress of adjusting early ideals to the opportunism and ego-centered requirements of "economic men."

The less successful or most ethically refined members of the learned professions—and the two are not always identical—are tempted to project any private sense of inadequacy upon society; they consider private capitalistic economics a corrosive enemy of devoted service to the public good. It would seem that intellectuals would be inclined by the detachment acquired in the pursuit of enlightenment to support bureaucratic forms rather than mixed business-bureaucratic forms of social organization. The orderly and nonacquisitive traits of a bureaucratic hierarchy do appeal to scholars, but the hierarchical principle is itself inimical to the untrammeled use of the mind, since it purports to stratify intellectuals by rank and grade. Scientific intellectuals are colleagues in pursuit of truths that are consensually valid; the discoverer of truth may be young or old, brilliant or slow, attractive or unattractive, healthy or ill, evil or good. There is basic equality among those who worship at the shrine of revelation and consult the sphinx with the secular or sacred rites of inquiry. There is also equality in the requirement of disclosure of information and interpretation. We conclude that the forum of the mind eventually dissolves hierarchy and is, in a deep sense, antibureaucratic; scholars are most comfortable in "coarchy," in a congregation whose affairs are handled by informal balloting based on intellectual merit. It is not "my authority" that settles "truth" in the commonwealth of mind; on the contrary "my accepted contribution" measures my authority.

As venerable as the scholarly tradition is, society probably has not yet found the social institutions most conducive to the cultivation of intellectual creativity. None of the forms employed to date are wholly adapted to the delicate poise of factors that affect the process. Not the forest of the solitary sage, nor the monastery, nor the circle

---

[12] For various leads to evaluation see E. M. Albert and C. Kluckhohn, *A Selected Bibliography on Values, Ethics and Esthetics* (Glencoe, Ill.: Free Press of Glencoe, Inc., 1959).

of an ambitious patron, nor the bureaucratic hierarchy of government and administration, nor the teaching college, nor the proliferated university, nor the specialized research bureau or center, nor the intermittent academy, nor the rough-and-tumble of the competitive market: none of these forms are wholly adequate, although all have been of historic importance in one context or another. In some historic or contemporary circumstances they have succumbed to degrees of corruptness and betrayed the fundamental and recurring requirements of creativity.[13]

At the moment the best prescription for the cultivation of enlightenment appears to be diversity of institutional forms. More particularly the present requirement is to counterbalance the heavy loading of factors that make for the culture of the mole by a combination of elements better adapted to further the culture of the mountain view.

Intellectuals have begun to adapt the corporate devices of capitalism to their own uses. The independent writer, painter, or historian who creates a popular form can become a rich man; and the mathematician, logician, physicist, chemist, biologist, psychologist, economist, political analyst, or sociologist who has a marketable product can organize a profit-making enterprise. The professional man or a small nucleus of professionals can join corporate organizations, share in the profits, and arrange to be relatively insulated against losses. A variety of mixed public and private organizations and profit and nonprofit organizations are emerging and obliterating traditional distinctions. Payment systems for managers, specialists, and consultants are linking income with the profit-and-loss position of the enterprise. The money from taxpayers is used to attract managerial and other talent by providing for a share in the benefits accruing to the total operation and by offering guarantees against loss. If the operation lacks capital, but still obtains general confidence, operating deficits are met, and the operation may be continued on an expanding scale.

The ductile practices of modern society are destroying well-estab-

<hr>

[13] For the history of universities and related institutions consult H. Rashdall, *The Universities of Europe in the Middle Ages* (new ed.; 3 vols.; New York: Oxford University Press, 1936). In more detail, H. D. Lasswell, *The Future of Political Science* (New York: Atherton Press, 1963).

lished distinctions between such categories as "profit" and "non-profit" or "private capitalist" and "public capitalist." A form of "ownership" or "management" no longer provides a simple clue to whether the public interest is well served or poorly served. The multi-valued consequences of every activity become more apparent as modern intellectual tools disclose how reverberation effects spread throughout the social process. Whether "socialism" or "capitalism" or "hierarchy" or "coarchy" serve the public interest depends upon the application of contextual analysis, and such application requires that a vast body of data be processed (presumably by computing machines) and that the results be made accessible to all who have the motivation and competence to understand.

The emerging map of society does not show that we are doing away with the tendencies of *some* social groups to get *more* of whatever social values there are. Human beings are re-creating the routines of civilization at such a rate that the *skill* revolution is at last emerging rather clearly into view and is superseding the simpler bipolar conception of a *class* struggle between "the rich" and "the poor." Modern societies reveal many gradations between top and bottom positions according to wealth, power, respect, enlightenment, skill, affection, rectitude, and well-being; the most advantaged participants are those who have the aptitude and opportunities to cultivate intellectual skills.[14]

The future impact of intellectuals depends upon whether or not the latter will bring up-to-the-minute maps of the social process into the choosing and deciding processes of society; such maps will make it possible to respecify goals and to apply maximizing criteria to the evaluation of policy alternatives. Any effect of "creeping" corruption will probably show itself in the form of omission rather than in the form of commission. It will continue to be easier to research and report on results that serve a definite and limited interest than to take on the complicated, often unrewarded task of appraising the common interest.

We entertain the sanguine view that intellectuals will perform the intelligence, recommending, and appraising functions with progressively greater effect. We need *independent* appraisals by com-

---

[14] See D. Marvick, ed., *The Decision-Makers* (Glencoe, Ill.: Free Press of Glencoe, Inc., 1961).

petent people who have adequate facilities. The idea of "the decision seminar" [15] outlines an institutional form adapted to the task of self-examination. Private scholars, whether working in universities, research institutes, or professional associations, can engage in continuing seminar operations that parallel the work of selected decision-making or choosing groups in society. Political scientists, for instance, can take responsibility for paralleling the trends and projections of the presidency, Congress, the courts, the party leaders, and the electorate; in doing so, they can seek to discover and display factors that account for past changes, to specify future objectives, and to invent and estimate future policy alternatives. Surrounded by a "chartroom" environment, which provides orientation through time, investigators can strive to bring the entire relevant configuration to the focus of attention and to participate in investigations designed to fill in gaps in knowledge. Economists can assume responsibility for paralleling choosers in the wealth process—bankers, manufacturers, trade unionists, consumers—and articulate postulates concerning aggregate goals. Social and behavioral scientists will probably perform similar tasks for every other value-institution process.

We have pointed out before how appropriate simulation can aid law enforcement. The present point is that the level of integrity of specialists depends upon subjecting skill to enlightenment and to the challenge of depicting the larger manifold of significant events. Corruption creeps in when specialists deliberately distort or are unwilling to arouse the resentment of and suffer reprisal from interests who feel endangered by aggregate presentations of the common interest.

Skill and the Institutions of Skill

Our examination of enlightenment has included many references to the skill value. It is pertinent to rectitude and power to take account of the amoral character so often shaped when there is great emphasis upon excellence. This also applies to the specialized cultivation of rectitude itself, since the time spent thinking about the limits of responsibility can often be spent in more responsible activity.

The cultivation of skill is accompanied by a degree of constriction or attrition of experience; the latter creates an aloofness that

---

[15] See H. D. Lasswell, "The Technique of Decision Seminars," *Midwest Journal of Political Science*, **4** (1960), 213-236.

arouses suspicion and resentment, since people feel more comfortable with spontaneous, though less refined, expressions. The creative mind and personality is elusive because that individual's focused motivation and capability result in a special map of the world. The immediate present—the "here and now"—is never fully lived in by the artist, poet, or thinker. No matter how deep the apparent involvement may appear to be at a given time, the response is disciplined by the standards of judgment that transcend the moment and point toward culminations. Potential culminations always affect the individual so long as the pursuit of excellence remains an active goal for him.

The most transparent connection between skill and corruption occurs when manifestly corrupt activities are raised to the level of a fine art. One does not hesitate to put the accomplished pickpocket, the skillful picker of safety locks, the talented poisoner, the specialist on unauthorized death by gun, knife, or paralyzing pressure in the guild of the corrupt. Many craftsmen have been devoted to the perfecting of fakes: false bills and notes; fake Michelangelos and Raphaels; false wills, passports, licenses, diplomas; false manuscripts; false anthropological specimens. Fakery of the kind is seldom profitable. It seems to depend upon a rebellious character formation conjoined with aptitude and taste. The need to make a fool of someone and to achieve a perverse sense of superiority accounts for much of the obsessional thoroughness of deceivers.[16]

The single-minded pursuit of scientific knowledge involves recurring temptations to transgress the limits of conventional propriety. Men and women who evaded the codes of decency of their society have learned much.[17] For instance nothing was more repugnant to religious and moral conviction than cutting up dead bodies; yet modern medicine would be unthinkable without cadavers to dissect. Animal vivisection has offended the conscience of millions; and artificial insemination of woman is a by-product of scientific work that has aroused indignant protest. It is seldom admitted that sexual intercourse is observed and recorded for scientific purposes or that infants, children, and young people are experimentally subjected to sexual stimulation. Anthropologists do not always report that their zeal for

---

[16] See O. Kurz, *Fakes: A Handbook for Collectors and Students* (New Haven: Yale University Press, 1948).

[17] Andrew D. White's *Warfare of Science and Religion* is a famous repository of pertinent material.

science led them to transcend the taboos of our civilization when they were on field trips among peoples of alien culture. The use of human beings, even with their consent, in dangerous experiments is vehemently opposed because it is a violation of human decency and because it is immoral to permit anyone to throw away his "natural right" to life.

The scientist is open to suspicion whenever he claims that breaching conventional morality is necessary to the common interest of enlightenment. Should such claims be considered valid? Or should they be critically evaluated by procedures that separate the advocate from the judge? Should we give automatic exemptions to any qualified scientist, no matter what his character may be? Despite all misgivings must we conclude that unrestrained research contributes more to human welfare than is possible when conventional moralists prohibit investigation?

The demand to transcend conventional morality to give full creative expression to talent is not new. "Science for the sake of science" parallels "art for art's sake" or any ideology that considers the claims of skill superior to the claims of any rival value, especially conventional morality.

Suppose, however, that the issue is joined, not at the level of automatic adherence to the local geography of morals, but at the level of conceptions of rectitude that affirm the dignity of man and require that motive and conduct be appraised in the context of all values affected. In this perspective what shall our conventional norms be? Who shall choose the norm and apply standards to concrete cases?

Questions of this kind will become more pressing rather than less pressing as knowledge of the social process cumulates and as new skill specialties multiply. Presumably we can count upon a rising level of skill to provide a basis of common experience that can be used to reach solutions. The informed examination of such issues will itself become a distinct skill; indeed that is an implication of the policy science conception.[18]

Respect and the Institutions of Respect

The respect institutions of American society are rapidly changing. The most obvious case is the liquidation of discriminations

---

[18] See D. Lerner and H. D. Lasswell, eds., *The Policy Sciences* (Stanford: Stanford University Press, 1951).

against Negroes. However this country has faced many campaigns of readjustment. Immigrants brought with them all the images and prejudices that were current in the cultures from which they came. If it was part of the tradition for Jews to look down upon Gentiles and Gentiles to look down upon Jews, these reciprocal distastes were transplanted to the New World.[19] If Protestants looked down upon Catholics and Catholics looked down upon Protestants, they continued to look askance at one another in this country. If noble lineage was treated deferentially in Europe, it continued to receive a measure of deference in America. Whatever the social images by which human beings succeeded in believing themselves inherently superior to their fellow men, these images were imported into the New World, aiding and abetting the general confusion of standards.

In the New World traditional lenses were cracked and broken, and people came to be more directly estimated in terms of individual merit. The process so persuasively described by de Tocqueville did not dissolve every bias nor prevent the development of novel discriminations; but the trend was unmistakable. The corrupting consequences of status-having gave way to the corruptions of status-seeking; in the long run the latter are competitive and self-correcting.

Since future immigration presumably will be highly restricted, a factor historically connected with corruption will play a role of diminishing importance. When immigrants are drawn from contrasting civilizations, conflicting norms often contribute to corrupt acts. When newcomers have little control over the social values that serve as important bases of action, they become targets of corrupt exploitation. The peasants and city workers who came to this country were usually poor, unskilled in the industrial arts, and unenlightened about American society. They needed orientation and, more important, an economic foothold. Frequently they suffered from unnecessarily burdensome exactions levied by recent immigrants and by corrupt Americans—politicians, labor organizers, employment agencies, and employers.

To some extent the exploitation of the newcomer was the self-protective response of those who considered the immigrants a threat to their own value position and preferred institutions. This was true

---

[19] Rich documentation is in Arnold A. Rogow, ed., *The Jew in a Gentile World* (New York: The Macmillan Company, 1961).

in every sector of life: in politics by the danger of "illiterate gangs" of foreigners to party ascendancy; in economics by the competitive menace of the "low standard of living" of the newcomer; in religion and morals by the onslaught of the "Catholic tradition" of middle and southeastern Europe; in family affairs by the alleged licentiousness and quarrelsomeness of immigrant households; in matters of hygiene by "dirty and diseased" foreigners; in standards of excellence by the clumsiness imputed to the stranger; in the demand for respectability by the lack of manners and the boorishness of the immigrant; in the demand for common enlightenment by the ignorance and seeming indifference of newcomers. Between the disadvantaged immigrant and the opportunities of the New World there evolved a specialized group of "fixers" who privately and secretively did what they would have been condemned for doing publicly and openly.

Immigration does not invariably breed corruption. The history of America provides many striking examples of transition with little or no temptation to act corruptly.[20] Some immigrant groups—notably the Japanese—continued to exercise collective control over their young people and thereby prevented disorganization. Once families and communities were established in the New World, the subculture was ready to contribute to the transition to American life. Many injustices to which immigrants were subjected were the result of the ignorance of Americans. American institutions of intelligence were too insufficiently evolved to provide a realistic program for the men of good will. Under present and prospective conditions future immigrants are likely to come under auspices that are substantially immune to corruption and that are professionally competent in administering programs of assimilation.

The preoccupation of Americans with the respect value is manifest in many ways: for example the increasing number of occasions for the awarding of honorary degrees, medals, ribbons, and certificates in recognition of longevity and endurance; the increasing number of testimonial dinners; and the ubiquitous snob appeals in advertising and merchandising and in general the attempt to accelerate obsolescence by the management of respect. Presumably the emphasis

---

[20] Oscar Handlin's *The American People in the Twentieth Century* (Cambridge: Harvard University Press, 1954) is an indispensable map.

upon respect will continue as inner-directed men give way to less obstinate types.[21]

We do not minimize the impact of scientific enlightenment upon respect. Technological change damages patterns of self-respect which are anchored to particular operations. Even more far-reaching is the challenge to man's self-regard that is epitomized in the displacement of man's habitat from the center of the astronomer's universe, in the attrition of man's claim to biological uniqueness by the concepts of evolution, or in the denial of the ascendancy of man's reason by the discovery of the unconscious. The distinction between "organic" and "inorganic" has wilted into a zone of equivocal forms. Subjective and nonsubjective events have become part of the same "manifold of events," among which operational distinctions may be made, not in principle, but according to convenient indices of "movement," "sign," and "symbol."

Practicing scientists or persons who are well-acquainted with science are not losing self-esteem. There is a mood of sustained excitement and pride among the thousands of men and women who have been actively engaged in or are most cognizant of the unfolding world of knowledge. Those who suffer from deflation of self-regard appear to be the bystanders and the uninformed; and with wider sharing of basic enlightenment the community at large will probably continue to respect those who contribute to enlightenment and demonstrate excellence.

Well-being and the Institutions of Safety, Health, and Comfort

Because of the threat of possible destruction, safety, health, and comfort are compromised by the conjuncture of factors which comprise the contemporary world order. Manifestations of individual insecurity are conspicuous features of the "Age of Anxiety." Although rates of neurosis appear to be rising, there are many offsetting trends; these range from the multiplication of chemical pacifiers for adults and children to new modes of diagnosing, treating, and preventing

---

[21] See A. J. Brodbeck, "Values in *The Lonely Crowd*: Ascent or Descent of Man?" S. M. Lipset and L. Lowenthal, eds., *Culture and Social Character; The Work of David Riesman Reviewed* (Glencoe, Ill.: Free Press of Glencoe, Inc., 1961), pp. 42-71.

personality disturbance. Undoubtedly such trends will continue until many, if not most, of the factors affecting disorder are recognized and controlled. In recent years we have learned that those who display deviational characteristics and who behave irresponsibly often are deeply disordered personalities. We are aware of the importance of distinguishing between "corrective" problems in the sanctioning policies of the community and "educative" problems. The former category includes all who require basic transformation before they can guide their conduct according to ordinary social rewards and penalties.[22]

In recent years the anxieties evoked by the spectacle of mental collapse have diverted attention away from the waste of human potential which results from failure to identify and cultivate individual capability. Partly because of the crisis of national security and especially because of the shift symbolized by Sputnik, national effort has turned toward remedying the anti-intellectualism of the past. An inventory of the relationship between latent capacity and effective opportunity has underlined the point that America has been running at low levels of efficiency. Many bright pupils do not continue their education, and those who do continue do not push ahead to reach levels of high competence.[23]

The neglect of intellectual capability has far-reaching results in personality integration. Many individuals of modest talent are pushed far beyond their optimum, and able people are condemned to frustrations that contribute to their demoralization and to social stresses and strains. Corruption as a blind protest against unrealized potentiality is beginning to emerge as an important factor. This problem, too, is open to continual investigation and correction.

Affection and the Institutions of Identity

Much of the disjointedness of complex social life is expressed in the sphere of sexual intimacy and friendship. The family institution

---

[22] See H. D. Lasswell and R. L. Donnelly, "The Continuing Debate over Responsibility: An Introduction to Isolating the Condemnation Sanction," *Yale Law Journal*, **68** (1959).

[23] On waste of potential consult National Manpower Council, *A Policy for Scientific and Professional Manpower* (New York: Columbia University Press, 1953); *Womanpower*, 1957; E. Ginzberg, *The Ineffective Soldier* (3 vols.; New York: Columbia University Press, 1959); E. P. Torrance, ed., *Talent and Education* (Minneapolis: University of Minnesota Press, 1960).

has been relieved of many social functions; today other circles are cultivated for the giving, receiving, and withholding of affection. The making and unmaking of marriages have grave consequences for adults and children, and there continues to be ample opportunity to appraise these delicate and subtle matters. We can safely forecast further concentration of talent upon the gradual clarification of workable goals in this area. With more investigation irresponsibility in these relations will be easier to identify and, once identified, easier to cope with.

Among the many implications of modern science for the future we underline the conflicts likely to be generated by greater freedom in the expression of affection. There is little ground for predicting that a single norm of sexual-intimate behavior can be enforced without multiplying the opportunities for blackmail, bribery, and corrupt administration. As sexuality is separated from fear of unwanted pregnancy or disease, the traditional deterrents lose much of their former significance. It has been suggested that a probable development is the reassertion of the repressed sexuality of mankind; namely, the proclivities of the polymorphous perverse.[24] Undoubtedly the norms of affection will be as open to chronic reconsideration in future years as they have been in the past.

Rectitude and the Institutions of Responsibility

When we deal directly with rectitude institutions, one of the first questions refers to organized religion. The long warfare between scientists and religionists has not ended, although there has been a reversal of influence in the last four centuries. Formerly ecclesiastics were able to require the scientists to defer to propositions affirmed by religionists; today most ecclesiastics claim that what they say is compatible with the affirmations of science and supplements them.

The ideologies of science once defended themselves from ecclesiastical attack by emphasizing an alleged distinction between truth by empirical observation and the "higher truths" of revelation. Today many ideologies of science are seeking a method of dispensing with "revelation" and of deriving goal values from empirical experience.

---

[24] Thoughtful formulations of collective psychopathology are N. Brown, *Life Against Death; The Psychoanalytical Meaning of History* (New York: Random House, 1959); H. Marcuse, *Eros and Civilization* (Boston: Beacon Press, 1955).

Theological statements about "God's plan" are treated as postulates from which empirically verifiable propositions have often been derived in the past. But many such hypotheses, it is asserted, are proved invalid by empirical observation and must be rejected as untenable. The original postulate must be either abandoned or re-edited.[25] The empiricists find no admitted place for "faith"; a working commitment to a postulate should not be confused with the intensity of conviction that is capable of leading men to disregard—to "transcend"—empirical knowledge. A "postulate" or "basic hypothesis" is not equivalent to a "doctrine" vouchsafed by "revelation" and "affirmed as faith."

How does the "empiricist" choose among hypotheses? One answer to this question is to put forward competing postulates, such as the affirmation that "man has an instinct to survive" or "the survival of the species works through individuals but through no particular individual." Statements of the kind are always open to the challenge —"Why choose that criterion?"

Our immediate purpose is served by pointing out the consequences of bringing the "concealed postulates" of "theologians" and "Messiahs" into the open as explicit "postulates." The social scientist asks, when any communication is made, "Who said what to whom in what channel to what audience with what effect?"; and no matter whether the statement is "empirical" or "transempirical" in reference ("manifest content"), the act of saying is still assessable in terms of its interaction with the shaping and sharing of values in the social context. The gap between persons who invoke the "transempirical" as a matter of faith and those who invoke "cosmic hypotheses" as matters of postulate may tactfully be ignored, but it is not likely to be bridged.

The disconcerting thought that "value commitments are matters of opinion" has been attacked as the source of all confusion and corruption in the life of man.[26] An answer satisfactory to many scientists is "of course"; but an "opinion" does not necessarily express an arbitrary impulse of the moment. A scientist makes responsible evalua-

[25] See A. Rapoport, *Operational Philosophy; Integrating Knowledge and Action* (New York: Harper & Row, Publishers, 1953); C. H. Waddington, *The Scientific Attitude* (2nd rev. ed.; Penguin Books, Inc., 1948).
[26] For a magistral review of this controversy see A. Brecht, *Political Theory; The Foundations of Twentieth-Century Political Thought* (Princeton: Princeton University Press, 1959).

tive commitments *after* he has subjected them to the discipline of considering all values at stake. The scientific mode of problem-solving disposes him to emphasize the *content* of statements as disciplined by *procedures* that bring the context into view.

If there is no world disaster, the scientific approach to the sifting of rival commitments will probably win out; hence science will provide the typical method of work employed by the ethicist or, more generally, the policy scientist. Our present developmental construct assumes no overwhelming disaster; and under less destructive contingencies earlier religious ideologies will probably be revived.

To speak of the revival of religion may seem strange, since organized religion often appears influential in contemporary affairs in the United States. However "church" institutions are subordinate to other social values. In cities, especially, churches are mild rectitude, respect, and affection institutions; they are only locally and sporadically capable of imposing the severe sanctions that once made ecclesiastical institutions effective institutions, although not necessarily authorized institutions, of power. (We are adhering to the analytical distinction between "conventionally labelled" institutions and "functionally analyzed" institutions, the latter being the analytic and empirical pictures painted by social scientists.) [27]

The former power of organized religion in American civilization and in western civilization can be detected in the role of *guilt* in personality systems. Guilt is an intense affirmation of a discrepancy between conduct and a rectitude norm. Guilt responses can be internalized; the self condemns the self. Judgments of guilt are also made of others. Such judgments are especially intense when they are unconscious projections of adverse appraisals of the self.

Probably one of the most important and conventionally disturbing results of modern research relates to guilt. Guilt often has immoral consequences. Instead of producing conformity to the norm that is ostensibly protected, the bludgeon of guilt may incapacitate the individual from living up to this norm or any other norm. Physicians see that guilt-generated conflicts precipitate psychotic disorder

---

[27] On religious organizations and practices see H. D. Lasswell and H. Cleveland, eds., *The Ethic of Power; The Interplay of Religion, Philosophy, and Politics* (New York: Harper & Row, Publishers, 1962); H. Cleveland and H. D. Lasswell, eds., *Ethics and Bigness; Scientific, Academic, Religious, Political, and Military* (New York: Harper & Row, Publishers, 1962).

or psychosomatic disease. They also discover that guilt leads to provocative conduct which is an unconscious strategy of bringing severe deprivations to bear against the self. The strategy of provocation—again without full conscious deliberation—is to induce guilt-generated conflict within the personality of the "other." The result may be punitive distortion of the norms that are ostensibly enforced. A "pair-situation" can be multiplied many times over as other participants who identify with the challenger or the challenged are drawn in.

Many corrupt practices of individuals who consider themselves relatively powerless spring from anxieties within the personality system. The offer of a propitiatory bribe or of sexual indulgence frequently expresses an exaggerated perception of the other person as a threat; and the exaggeration arises from the conflict between impulses to fight back and the self-opprobrium imposed upon the self by the norm of nonresistance to an officer.[28]

A parallel point arises in the case of individuals who feel they are powerful. Guilt from the exercise of power can lead to overindulgences (e.g., jobs and favors) which are clear violations of responsibility.

The blind and archaic role of guilt probably will be attenuated gradually. The uprooting of guilt will depend upon remodeling the practices of socialization in ways that prevent the learning of guilt responses or the fixing of unlearned patterns of guilt. The elimination of guilt is a precondition of more responsible conduct in setting norms and in abiding by their requirements.

---

[28] See H. D. Lasswell, "Bribery," *Encyclopaedia of The Social Sciences,* **2,** 690-692.

Chapter Five

Ideology, Strategy, and Rectitude

Is American Ideology Extinct?

Any glimpse of the future requires an assessment of the validity of the assertion that ideologies are vanishing from the roster of effective influences in the United States. The proposition is usually supported by factual affirmations about the epoch as a whole and especially about the plight of youth, who presumably experience the characteristic impact of the period with maximum intensity. We speak of the world "Crisis of Insecurity," the "Age of Anxiety," or even the "Age of Kafka." Young people, it is alleged, are utterly confused about the goals of life. They lack identity; they are unable to delimit or to submerge the boundaries of the primary ego and therefore are incapable of achieving an inclusive self. They are desperately apprehensive and apathetic about public affairs and are vulnerable to the corrupting effects of noncommitment.[1]

The evidence cited to support the contention that ideology is losing its grip usually begins with information about juvenile delinquency. If we take the year 1940 as the base, the number of juveniles (the ages 10 to 17) in the population of the United States dropped off slightly and did not exceed the 1940 figure until 1954. However

---

[1] See D. Bell, *End of Ideology* (Glencoe, Ill.: Free Press of Glencoe, Inc., 1960); J. Talmon, *Political Messianism; The Romantic Phase* (New York: Frederick A. Praeger, Inc., 1960).

the curve of juvenile court cases rose during the war, declined briefly, and then rose steadily; by 1954 the volume of such cases was twice the flow of 1940.[2]

We can understand the social setting of these cases when we compare the size of the communities served by the courts. The highest rate per thousand juvenile population (35.1) is in the communities of 100,000 and over. This rate drops off to 5.5 in communities under 5,000. If juvenile delinquency is accepted as an indication of failure to socialize the rising generation, then the larger the community the greater the failure.

Ever since scholars became concerned with the alleged alienation of man from culture, a great deal of emphasis has been put upon the phenomenon of suicide. When the late President Thomas G. Masaryk of Czechoslovakia was a young sociologist, he used the available figures to demonstrate that the ideological cleavages of urbanization and the Protestant Reformation were critical events in disorganizing modern men.[3] Durkheim pointed to social environments which appeared to foster the voluntary resignation of life. It is consonant with Durkheim's expectations to find that the incidence of suicide in this country is higher among single people than among married people and that single people are excelled by the widowed and the divorced.[4] It is easy to suggest, but difficult to establish, that the suicide-prone tend to alienate others before they alienate themselves and that the critical predispositions are organized in early interaction with family members.

However there are interesting indications on a comparative basis of "cultural identification" with the body politic. The Americans and the Australians have an optimistic view of their own countries. An interview question in 1953 was: "Which country in the world gives you the best chance of leading the kind of life you would like to lead?" Eighty-two per cent of the Australians and 97 per cent of the

---

[2] See S. Glueck, ed., *The Problem of Delinquency* (Boston: Houghton Mifflin Company, 1959); P. W. Tappan, *Crime, Justice, and Correction* (New York: McGraw-Hill Book Company, Inc., 1960.

[3] T. G. Masaryk, *Der Selbstmord als Sociale Massenerscheinung der Modernen Civilisation* (Vienna, 1881).

[4] A. F. Henry and J. F. Short, *Suicide and Homicide* (Glencoe, Ill.: Free Press of Glencoe, Inc., 1954).

Americans named their respective nations. Thirty per cent of the Germans and the Dutch named their own countries.[5]

One objection has been that asking about "the kind of life you would like" is very different from confronting an individual with a vivid picture of the sacrifices that he may be asked to make. Did not the record of American soldiers in the Korean War illustrate the shallowness of American identifications?

The significance of Korea is variously interpreted by competent persons. Many units of the early contingents were catapulted into action without adequate technical training in the arts of war. Even well-trained units were conspicuously unindoctrinated about the national interest which they were asked to support with their lives if necessary. They soon realized that they were the front line of a divided nation, but they were ignorant of available alternatives of policy. There was minimum preparation of American soldiers to meet the strategies of ideological warfare adapted to military prisoners. No matter how we construe the results of the Korean campaign and its aftermath, they were experienced as a blow, like Sputnik, to a fantastical image of the American self in the arena of global power.[6]

Delinquency figures call attention to the disorganized state of the great metropolitan core areas. A caricature suggests that anyone who is relatively American, middle- or upper-income, and white flees to suburbia, leaving the debilitated capital equipment of the ancient urban center to the Puerto Ricans, the Negroes, the Mexicans, and the poor whites. Despite generations of experience in assimilating millions of our forefathers, contemporary American society has neglected to open the door of opportunity and of ideological-cultural incorporation to the current wave of arrivals. Only a trickle of newcomers from Europe have received the specialized attention required to ease the cost of transition.

The clashes in many metropolitan districts are not between totally isolated individuals; they are the fighting front of larger iden-

---

[5] W. Buchanan and H. Cantril, *How Nations See Each Other: A Study of Public Opinion* (Urbana, Ill.: University of Illinois Press, 1953).

[6] Concerning the strategy of disintegration see R. J. Lifton, *Thought Reform and The Psychology of Totalism* (New York: W. W. Norton & Company, Inc., 1961); R. Hunter, *Brain-Washing in Red China* (New York: Vanguard Press, 1951).

tities engaged in adjusting, however clumsily, to one another and to an inhospitable local environment. As we remarked before, there are signs that restorative operations are going forward and that American financial, commercial, industrial, political, and cultural leaders are finally rallying to meet the metropolitan problems that beset the nation.

Social scientists are beginning to revise their outlook concerning isolation—an outlook which was insisted upon by nineteenth century and early twentieth century students of urbanism. The rootless bum is neither the average, the median, nor the "ideal" metropolitan type. Research is demonstrating the point that the city, like the town, is a pattern of interlocking territorial and plural groupings. Even the bums congregate. But the structure of society runs along kinship, ethnic, skill, and many related lines. A study in Los Angeles, for example, shows that family visiting accounts for a large part of the weekend social life of the urbanite. At one time the case for vanishing ideology was made by citing the rootless proletarian. Today the complaint appears to be that people are so determinedly rooted in small-group affairs that they are minimally involved in the larger ideological and institutional configurations of the age.[7]

The evidence mentioned so far to support the thesis of ideological decline is not convincing. Perhaps we should underscore the point that we do *not* confine the meaning of the term *ideology* to stable perspectives whose adherents can provide a well-systematized exposition of the doctrine. Many people complain that the difficulty which American students have in outarguing Communist-indoctrinated students demonstrates that American ideology has lost its grip. We do not care to limit the definition this drastically. Glibness in presenting systematic doctrine is not characteristic of many pious members of religious faiths, for example, and we see no advantage in excluding

---

[7] See M. J. Janowitz, ed., *Community Political Systems* (Glencoe, Ill.: Free Press of Glencoe, Inc., 1961); R. H. Smuckler and G. M. Belnap, *Leadership and Participation in Urban Affairs*, Governmental Research Bureau, Political Research Studies No. 2 (East Lansing, Michigan: Michigan State University Press, 1956); A. Vidich and J. Bensman, *Small Town in Mass Society* (Princeton: Princeton University Press, 1958); R. Young, ed., *Approaches to the Study of Politics* (Evanston: Northwestern University Press, 1958), Part 4, contributions by G. W. Blackwell, A. Campbell, S. Greer., F. Hunter, and P. H. Rossi; M. R. Stein, *The Eclipse of Community* (Princeton: Princeton University Press, 1961).

the inarticulately devout by definition from the rank of believers. It is more conducive to inquiry if research is directed to discover who becomes articulate and to ascertain whether variations of articulateness predict courage to endure severe deprivations on behalf of beliefs. We define ideology to include a considerable degree of commitment on the part of most members of a group; we refer to a nuclear commitment rather than a peripheral commitment of the individuals involved.

Given the fragmentary knowledge now at hand concerning ideology in America, what conclusions—subject to correction by further inquiry—can we make about the occurrence and strength of ideology and the prospects that noninvolvement will be sufficient to breed corruptions? Note that the strength of an ideology is to be estimated in terms of its capability to maintain and extend effective influence over conduct. This can be estimated according to the number of people affected and the scope and range of impact upon each individual and situation.

Our interpretation is that the ideology of human dignity is very strong in American civilization and that much of the confusion, uncertainty, conflict—even corruption—characteristic of American life is due to the vitality of our ideological orientation. The conception of the worth of individuality, and of the obligation to correct whatever stands in the way of a social order based upon merit, is sufficiently potent to maintain a continuing stress toward self-appraisal and to inspire the perpetual reconstruction of American personality and culture in accord with ideal aspirations toward human dignity.

The traditional ideology of America provides a problem-solving guide. The goal of realizing a commonwealth in which "life, liberty and pursuit of happiness" is taken seriously in theory and fact provides a frame of reference for the examination of the past and probable future and for the invention and evaluation of proposed alternatives of public and individual policy. More concretely an ideology aids problem-solving by fostering the performance of five intellectual tasks: the clarification of *goal*; the description of *trends* in the degree to which goal values are achieved; the analysis of *conditioning factors*; the *projection* of future developments; and the invention and evaluation of *policy alternatives* by which preferred outcomes (the goal events) can be maximized.

In this connection it is helpful to emphasize the distinction between social process in value terms and process in terms of patterns relatively specialized to value-shaping and value-sharing (institutions).

We have said that to affirm human dignity is to proclaim commitment to the goal of a society in which value outcomes are widely rather than narrowly participated in. Hence aspiration in terms of power is for democratic rather than for nondemocratic institutions of government; in terms of wealth, for graduated income classes rather than for sharp separation between a wealthy few and a poverty-stricken many; in respect terms, for social classes rather than for castes; in enlightenment matters, for general access to news and information; in regard to skill, for wide opportunity to mature socially contributory capability; in the sphere of affection, for congeniality and warmth in human relationships; in the area of well-being, for widespread sharing of safety, health, and comfort; in regard to rectitude, for the cultivation of a sense of individual responsibility for evaluating all personal or collective policies in terms of their compatibility with the goal of human dignity.

To commit one's ego or all the members of a group to an ideal goal does not provide a final solution for the problems of living. Common cultural backgrounds provide a degree of consensus as to the specific practices compatible with, and contributory to the overriding goal. However consensus is far from complete; in a complex and rapidly evolving society there is uncertainty about many specific interpretations of objective and about policies best adapted to the contingent future. The choosing processes throughout society must therefore be adapted to the task of clarifying specific objectives and of selecting courses of action that expedite the objectives.

The ideology of human dignity not only provides a guide to thinking about goals, but also furnishes a guide to procedures by which thinking can be done with the promise of discovering workable solutions that facilitate the goal. In short, ideology includes principles of *content* and *procedure*. Principles of content enable us to distinguish goals of human dignity *versus* human indignity; principles of procedure indicate how to increase the likelihood that the choices we make will implement the goals that we proclaim.

In a fundamental sense we can say that the vitality of American

ideology is exhibited not in the elaboration of definitions and justifications of goal, but in discovering operational arrangements which
enable us to invent and recognize measures that harmonize with our
aspirations.
    Americans—and especially young people—are not unwilling to
concern themselves with serious reading on ideological matters.
Serious reading is not a sign of apathy; it shows a concern with basic
issues. Today's volume of serious publication and reading is impres-
sive. Consider the paperbacks. It is famous in the trade that "heavy"
titles sell, and publishers who have feather-down material on their
hard-cover list must ferret out suitable additions to their paperbacks.
And who reads the "paper heavies"? Young people—especially young
people in college or in graduate and professional school and recently
appointed faculty. (This is obviously the reading hour on the clock-
face of life.)
    The shelves pullulate with vivid exposition and controversy in
every precinct of human affairs. Consider theology and morals.
Among contemporary Protestant theologians—and it must be con-
ceded that Protestant theology has become intellectually reputable
once more—are Barth, Niebuhr, and Tillich. Neo-Thomists are richly
represented. The rising curve of interest in oriental theology is expressed, for example, in expositions of Zen Buddhism. On every shelf
is a lengthened shadow of Sartre.
    The world of secular enlightenment is represented by scientists
and scholars from the physical, biological, and social sciences and the
humanities. The breakdown of the mechanical view of causation with
the advent of the principle of uncertainty or complementarity is read-
ily available in the words of great innovators like Planck, Schrödinger,
and Heisenberg. The once-rigid frame of particles and energies has
dissolved in Einstein's equivalency of mass and energy, and there are
explanations of relativity by, and with the aid of, Einstein. The map
of the galaxies has spectacularly unfolded with the advent of big lenses
and radio astronomy and with cosmological hypotheses of an expanding or contracting universe. Harlow Shapley and his colleagues are
among those who have reached a wide lay audience with this material. Rigid boundaries between "organic" and "inorganic" gave way
when Wendell Stanley convinced fellow chemists and physicists that
a certain tobacco mold was "both" or "neither," and biology is

heavily represented in the paperbacks. The adventures of living forms and of man are depicted by Childe, Linton, and Toynbee. Maps of the social process appear in the older version of Marx, in more modern editions of Weber and Durkheim, and in contemporary formulations from many hands. Men of science and religion, notably Chardin, have produced bold intellectual models and declarations of commitment which are accessible to anyone.

In the realm of the expressive arts some writers have successfully portrayed the beauties and horrors, the horizons and the limits of a man who is increasingly manipulative and possessed of formidable capabilities for manipulation. Think of the vogue of Aldous Huxley, Koestler, Orwell, and Snow. And there are men highly specialized to particular skills who seek to share their vision of potential application with their fellow men. See, for an example, Skinner's *Walden Two* where "happiness" is pushed by modern-minded indoctrinators.

The cruciality of the shaping and sharing of economic outcomes for the welfare of the modern world is generally recognized. Hence special importance is attached to treatises such as Keynes's *General Theory*, because they set the terms of recent thought about production, saving, investment, and consumption. Today anti-Keynes forces are again alert in view of problems connected with inflation, economic growth, exchange frictions, and unemployment.[8]

In many ways the most successful attempts to provide a popular political theory have come from economists and lawyers who have been abundantly exposed to policy responsibility. We refer, for example, to Galbraith's modernization of the Federalist principle of countervailing power. There are, of course, controversies phrased in terms of "conservatism," old or new, or "liberalism," equally old or new.

Perhaps the most provocative contribution on matters relating to the stratification of respect are the many volumes of Lloyd Warner and his associates. Lives there an American so benighted that he remains in doubt about his "U" or "non-U" status? (If so, he is triple "U" or triple "L," and imagination boggles at the thought.) There is also the effort to deflate racist ideologies—a task to which the late Ruth Benedict, whose main contribution was in another area, sapiently attached so much importance.

---

[8] See H. Hazlitt, *The Critics of Keynesian Economics* (Princeton: D. Van Nostrand Co., Inc., 1960).

On matters pertaining to affection and especially to familial practices the roster of impactful figures is very long indeed.

When we come directly to somatic and psychic integrity, the galaxy is rich and full: Freud, Sullivan, Horney, Jung, and Adler are only a few of the innovators and contributors.

Serious reading is one of the many signs of intellectual concern with fundamental issues. In the course of this book we have noted the dynamic interplay between many values and also between norms and behavior.

The essential conclusion regarding the ideology of human dignity is that the ideology is strong among us because it provides a built-in challenge to scrutinize individual and group practices from the point of view of the contributions they make, or fail to make, to the goal. This challenge is a corrosive and creative component of individual personality and of the culture of every subgroup in American society. This built-in component sooner or later challenges undemocratic practice in government and the economy: it makes caste take the defensive; it distrusts and challenges secrecy and all measures that deny public enlightenment; it indicts every obstacle in the path of capability; it questions every ritualized claim to rectitude and demands that it be revalidated in terms of the whole of human experience; it challenges every convention regarding intimacy and friendship; it demands, in the sphere of well-being for example, that physicians, too, subject themselves to unrelenting and intermittent scrutiny in terms of all the values of human dignity.[9]

Does this constituent of culture—the ideology of human dignity —create complacency, conformity, and quiet? Indeed not; and the psychic and other costs to the complacent, the conformist, and the inert are among the factors that contribute to the complaint—an impression far from justified—that ideology is extinct. It will not be extinct until it has brought about more-sweeping conformity between its requirements and the institutional arrangements of our society, or

---

[9] M. Jones and others, *The Therapeutic Community* (New York: Basic Books, Inc., 1953); M. Greenblatt, D. J. Levinson, R. H. Williams, eds., *The Patient and the Mental Hospital* (Glencoe, Ill.: Free Press of Glencoe, Inc., 1957); A. H. Leighton, J. A. Clausen, R. N. Wilson, eds., *Explorations in Social Psychiatry* (New York: Basic Books, Inc., 1957); W. Caudill, *The Psychiatric Hospital As a Small Society* (Cambridge, Mass.: Harvard University Press, 1958).

until it has been successfully rejected by those who find that ideologies of caste are more compatible with their drives and opportunities.

The Strategy of Harmonizing Rectitude and Power

The foregoing pages have primarily dealt with projections of the future, freely admitting the shadows that the future holds for the fate of the fundamental goals that we share with fellow Americans who identify themselves with the high aspirations of the great tradition. We have made rather incidental reference to policies which, if supported, would diminish corruption in various circumstances. We have yet to discuss more directly and systematically a strategy of action designed to reconcile power and rectitude in coming years.

We consider strategy in terms of sanction; that is, in the context of measures designed to encourage conformity and to discourage violation of norms of responsible conduct. Sanction strategy seeks to provide a body of guiding principles for the choice of patterns of value deprivation and value indulgence and to specify practices that most effectively apply these positive and negative sanctions.

More concretely the strategy of sanction within any system of public order is accomplished by resort to the legal system and also by reliance upon civic arrangements. For the purposes of comparative political science and jurisprudence we reserve the term *law* to refer to institutional practices which are authoritative and controlling and involve severe rather than mild deprivations. In the "civic order," when deprivations are employed at all, they are relatively mild.

The reason for distinguishing between public order and civic order is to enable us to describe important likenesses and differences between conventional systems. For instance the city government of Chicago or indeed the Congress of the United States passes two varieties of ordinances and statutes. Some prescriptions, when violated, are expected to be sanctioned by the use of severe value deprivations directed at offenders. Other prescriptions have no sanctioning provisions or, at most, are expected to involve light fines or expressions of censure. By distinguishing between the public and civic systems of order, we can, after appropriate inquiry, describe the functional significance of whatever institutions are locally called governmental. When we analyze other institutions—institutions locally called by some other name—functional analysis is capable of yielding important results. When we examine big business or big unions, for example, we find that the sanctioning norms applied to their members or to others are also severe or mild. Investigation may show that these institutions bearing conventional labels like "corporation" or "union" do in fact perform many power functions, which they may or may not be formally authorized by the community to carry on.

Within the membership context of any value-institution process (e.g., "church," "lodge," "family," "hospital," "university," "art association,") we can classify sanctions by degree of severity and mildness from the point of view of the membership. We can classify the same sanctions as they are viewed within the wider context of the entire community. Both modes of classification are appropriate for various purposes.

When we speak of a fully stated legal norm, we are referring to a prescription having three components: (1) a statement of factual contingency; (2) a statement of primary norm applicable to the participants in the circumstances; (3) a statement of the secondary (sanctioning) norm. The same categories apply to norms other than legal prescriptions. Consider, for example, the norms that may or may not be fully articulate in a family, but which can be described by a competent observer of family behavior. A simple prescription may be addressed to the children: When money belongs to somebody else (contingency), don't take it (primary norm); if you do, you will be spanked (sanctioning norm).

Our special problem within the vast field of sanction strategy is with the measures whereby corruption can be eliminated or at least reduced and correctness can be brought to or kept at high levels. Whether we have in mind power in conventional institutions of government or power in any other institution, the same five objectives of strategy can be identified.

The objective of *prevention* is to diminish the occasions which make corruption tempting and to manage the socialization and assimilation processes of society in such a way that tempting occasions are not seized. An example of the former—the elimination of provocation—is the cutting down of the cash at the disposal of cashiers. An example of the latter is the stressing of money honesty in home and school.

The objective of *deterrence* is to cut down corruption by em-

phasizing the probable cost of violating a norm. The sight of police-
men patrolling a beat is supposed to deter deviational acts by remind-
ing anyone who is tempted that he probably will be detected and
dealt with.

The objective of *restoration* is to bring a situation back, if possible, to the state of affairs that existed before a deviational act was
performed. Sometimes this is a simple matter of undoing; for example returning the stolen funds or getting off the property that is il-
licitly entered.

The objective of *rehabilitation* is to repair damage that presents
a problem too complex for restoration to put right. The license which
has been corruptly issued may have put firearms in the hands of a
person who kills another. Although it is impossible to undo the ultimate deprivation of death, it is possible to make provision for alleviat-
ing the plight of the widow and her children.

The objective of *reconstruction* is to alter the fundamental patterns of a situation or a personality and thereby, in this case, reduce
future corruption. Reconstruction thus differs from prevention in
scope of the changes sought. To reconstruct is to step outside established perspectives and operations and to introduce far-reaching practices, such as the collective liability of a family for damages committed by adult members. The latter is a very old practice and one
that the growth of individual liability in our history was designed to
supersede. If it were reintroduced or modified to acknowledge collective liability of an organization (even a government) for the acts of
its employees, the change would be considerable.

For the accomplishment of these objectives *all* social values are,
to some extent, available to public officials or private persons. Obviously each value may be used indulgently or deprivationally. The
stock instance is wealth: we levy fines, or we offer bonuses. Consider
respect: we honor someone, or we treat him with contempt. Or rectitude: we declare him innocent of wrongdoing, or we stigmatize him
as immoral. Similarly with affection: we reward with love, and we
punish with indifference. And enlightenment: we communicate, or we
withhold. Or skill: we allow training, or we block it. Or well-being: we
give extra food and luxurious lodging, or we cut down food and accom-
modations. And power: we continue in office, or we throw the rascal
out. (Observe that this illustration of power is in terms of a conven-

tional institution—an office.) In the most comprehensive functional sense power designates every severe value deprivation or threat. It is employed as an indulgence when, for instance, the control of severe deprivation is shared. When an offender is compelled to do hard labor, the deprivation is in terms of well-being. It is also in terms of power when the labor is considered a severe rather than a mild deprivation.[10]

From the point of view of the responsibility of a target, sanction measures are *educational* or *corrective*. When people are able to calculate risks and to control their own behavior according to the standards of a cultural context, they are *responsible*. When they are unable to calculate risks up to a standard minimum level, they are *not responsible*. Individuals in the latter category are corrective problems, since they are unable to learn from the ordinary life of society. They require reconstruction if they are to achieve this level. Obviously the skills available at any given time may not be enough to achieve reconstruction. If they are not, it may be necessary to adopt the time-honored device of protecting public order by removing the individual permanently from everyday association with it. Today the advances of chemical and communication therapies are such that the prospects for future strategies of coping with individual offenders are good.

Entire groups also require reconstruction, but this is rarely possible on a large scale—for nation-states, for example. Only in such critical situations as social revolution and defeat in war are circumstances propitious for sweeping transformations. However, in modern societies the tempo of change has accelerated and may be expected to increase until the new age of science and technology has been stabilized.[11]

Conclusion

We conclude our examination of power and rectitude by summarizing the course that we have followed. The Acton principle that

---

[10] As a formal matter of procedure we do not double-classify. Hence mildly deprivational labor is called well-being; when severe, the situation is called a power relation that employs well-being as an additional base in the context of relevant interaction. The basic distinctions are in H. D. Lasswell and A. Kaplan, *Power and Society* (New Haven: Yale University Press, 1950).

[11] M. S. McDougal and F. P. Feliciano, *Law and Minimum World Public Order: The Legal Regulation of International Coercion* (New Haven: Yale University Press, 1961).

"power tends to corrupt . . ." was already part of the inheritance of the Americans who drafted the Constitution and launched the nation. The aphorism condensed in a vivid slogan the latent and often manifest rejection of power which was embedded in the political perspectives of Christendom. In the environment of the New World American political institutions were designed and launched with the demand to curb public or private concentrations of power; more specifically the nation began with a self-consciousness of the potential abuses of authority by government. Hence our institutions were developed on the assumption that democracy depended upon a strategy of balancing structure against structure at every level. Our first task was to sum up the subsequent political experience of the nation and to show that the strategy has had grave, adverse consequences for the body politic at home and abroad.

The second task was to deal directly with the Acton principle by subjecting it to two tests—the biographical test and the institutional test. In the former test public men who experienced a rapid rise or fall in power were selected. The institutional test was brief, but also telling; it examined the record for corruption or correctness among those who were responsible for strong or weak organs of government. Both tests, although applied in preliminary fashion, point strongly to the view that power has no necessary impact upon rectitude.

Since we recognized that impact depends upon a context of factors rather than upon any simple connection between power and rectitude, our last step was to draw up a theoretical model which calls attention to contexts in which power leads to corruption or ennoblement.

With present-day trend and factor knowledge in view we went ahead to construct a developmental model concerning the future of corruption in America. Every value-institution process was taken into account in examining the probable structure of coming events.

Although the present treatment of a rich and much neglected field is brief, we believe that the following conclusions are warranted: (a) the growth of proper strategy for the exercise of shared power in America and by Americans has been held back as a result of the approach to politics crystallized in the Acton principle; (b) the Acton assertion that "power tends to corrupt . . ." is a gross oversimplification of the facts, since power also ennobles and powerlessness also corrupts or ennobles; and (c) the method of political thought exemplified by Acton is exceedingly inappropriate to the examination of politics.

We affirm that the proper method is the contextual method, which recognizes that every problem demands the performance of at least five intellectual tasks. In the case of the problem of power and rectitude, for example, goals regarding value outcomes must be respecified through time. Trends in the history of the American commonwealth require careful study to keep the dimensions of the problem in mind and to disclose the changing constellation of conditioning factors that determine the effect of power. The contextual method also requires that the probable order of future events be projected and that, when the picture is built up, policy implications for a corruption-free America receive imaginative and critical evaluation.

Appendix

A Note on Definition

A positively responsible act serves a system of public or civic order coextensive with a community context. *Deviations* from the norms of public and civic order are *negatively responsible acts* when they are performed by persons capable of education and exposed to the opportunity of acquiring the relevant norms. We say that the citizen of a democratic polity is acting in a positively responsible manner when he strives to protect the fundamental institutions and the basic pattern of value distribution within the commonwealth.

In a world of conflicting systems of public order scientific or lay observers are aware that responsible acts often conflict with one another. Thus those who are identified with public order *A* regard its spies abroad as engaged in highly responsible acts. In the perspective of public order *B*, of course, the same actors and activity are destructive.

We define a *subversive act* as a violation of responsibility toward one public or civic order on behalf of another with which the actor is actually, although not necessarily formally, identified.

A *corrupt act* violates responsibility toward at least one system of public or civic order and is in fact incompatible with (destructive of) any such system. A system of public or civic order exalts common interest over special interest; violations of the common interest for special advantage are corrupt.

132

In applying these distinctions, we bear in mind the difference between *conventional* and *functional* definitions. The former exist in the usage of a particular social context, such as the United States at a given period. Functional distinctions are made for scholarly and scientific purposes; ultimately they have in view all social contexts and hence define terms for comparative analysis.

Consider the phenomenon of "bribery." In functional terms we say that bribery is corrupt, since it is destructive of public order for anyone to tender or receive an inducement for the purpose of promoting special interest above common interest. Conventionally, however, the prescriptions of various public and civic systems may diverge greatly from one another. The legal code may seek to reach only the bribe-taker and leave the bribe-giver or offerer alone. In some communities only "extreme" payments or offers are considered threats to the common interest; elsewhere any payment may be forbidden.

Among many Americans bribery has the conventional connotation that wealth is involved. Our functional system of analysis, however, allows for the possibility that the inducement given or sought makes use of other values, such as power (e.g., a higher office or a voice in party councils), respect (e.g., favorable publicity), well-being (e.g., luxurious entertainment), affection (e.g., acceptance in a family circle), enlightenment (e.g., inside dope), skill (e.g., access to advanced training), and rectitude (e.g., moral support from a cynical group).

An important and presently unsettled question is: Do all societies, whether civilizations or folk cultures, possess norms that prohibit bribery? So far as folk societies are known, the evidence is sometimes obscure, partly because of the difficulty in equating the norms of "kinship and local" systems with state systems.

Bribery is an instance of expected or realized *value gain* in a corrupt act. Some corruption proceeds, not by inducement, but by creating an expectation or realization of *avoided loss*. All values may be at stake, since corruption may be engaged in to avoid foreclosure of mortgage (wealth), to prevent a political boss from blocking renomination (power), to preclude blackmail (respect and rectitude), to avoid being beaten up (well-being), to prevent exclusion from inside information (enlightenment), to prevent disqualification as a candidate for further training and competition (skill), or to forestall loss of friends (affection).

The various participations in a sequence of corrupt conduct may have very similar or very different perspectives in regard to their own goal values.

The strategies of those who initiate a corrupt sequence of conduct are aimed at affecting expectations of gain or loss. In this context we note that expectations may be influenced by all the *instruments* of policy at the disposal of participants in the political process. Following usage, we may classify these instruments according to the degree of reliance upon symbols and signs or according to the degree of nonsign resources. *Communication* and *diplomacy* rely characteristically upon symbols and signs—the former addressing all members of the body politic, and the latter focusing upon negotiation with elites. *Economic* and *military* instruments use resources that are specialized to production or to destruction (weapons). Obviously the strategies employed may be largely *persuasive* or *coercive*. If the strategies are persuasive, the target has relatively advantageous alternative outcomes at low cost; if the strategies are coercive, he has relatively deprivational alternative outcomes at high cost.

Many other distinctions can be made for various purposes; for the present, however, it is sufficient to note the familiar difference between *commission* and *omission*.

Index

Academic community, 101
Acton principle:
  adverse consequences of, 1, 2, 32, 130
  aphorism stated, 3, 4
  biographical test of, 33-55, 130
  conclusions with reference to, 130, 131
  embedded in political perspective of Christendom, 5, 6, 130
  institutional test of, 55-64, 130
  lack of contextuality, 65
  part of social inheritance of drafters of the Constitution, 7, 130
  question of validity of, 32, 65
Advocacy and judgment, 88, 89
Affection and the institutions of identity, 112, 113, 128, 133
"Age of Anxiety," 111, 117
Agencies, multiplication of, 23
Alienation of man from culture, 118
Ambivalent class perspective toward elites, 102
Antibusiness ideologies, 99
Anti-intellectualism, 112
Antimonopoly program, 94
Antitrust programs, 94
Anxieties within personality system, 116
Appraisal function in government, 87, 105, 106
Appraiser, independence of, 87
Arthur, Chester A., 36, 37
Articles of Confederation, 7, 9, 10, 14
Atomic Energy Commission, 25

Behavior of power-possessors, 32
Behavioral scientists, 106
Betrayal of confidence, 73
Bias in favor of the "Left," 102
Biographical test of Acton principle, 33-55, 130
Bipartisanship, 25
Bosses and political machines, 22 (see also Political bosses)
Bribery, 94, 133
Brigandage and economics, 94, 95
Bureaucratic state, 99
Bureaucrats, 31, 84
Burr, Aaron, 41-44
Business:
  fate of as social institution, 99
  moralistic attacks against, 98, 99
  public policy toward, 94

"Center" mechanism, 100, 101
Centralization at federal level:
  for security considerations, 78
  of state and municipal financing, 79

Centralized government, 83
Challenge:
  of the truth of the Acton principle, 1
  of undemocratic practice in government and the economy, 125
Change:
  acceleration in modern societies, 129
  as related to corruption, 70
Church institutions, 115
Civic order, sanction strategy within, 126
Civic responsibility, 76, 92
Civil rights for minorities, 29
Class struggle, 105
Coalition politics, 19
"Coarchy," 103
Colonialism, 76
Commissions, regulatory, 23, 24
  "life cycle" of, 60
Competition transformed into monopoly, 93, 94
Computer revolution, 81, 101
Conflicts:
  between executive and legislative branches, 18
  generated by greater freedom in expression of affection, 113
Congress:
  decline of prestige after Civil War, 61
  indifference to corrupt behavior of members, 61
Conscious perspectives, 73
Conservatism, 124
Consolidated government, 9, 10
Constitution, the, 7, 12, 14, 15, 17, 24, 26, 27
  amendments to, 17
  checks and balances in, 15, 16
  and restrictions on power, 15
  power divided among agencies, 16, 17
Constitutional convention, 10-12, 14, 15
Contextual approach, 66, 83, 131
"Conventional" definitions, 133
Coordinator, or "fixer," 22
Corrupt act, 132
Corruption:
  conditioned by "capability" as well as by "perspectives," 74
  definitions of, 2
  degrees of, 68
  and desire for personal gain, 2
  explanation of, 54
  fluctuating trends in, 66
  in the Grant and Harding administrations, 57
  and immigration, 109, 110

135